SOUTH CAROLINA

MORE DAILY DEVOTIONS FOR DIE-HARD FANS

GAMECOCKS

MORE SOUTH CAROLINA

More Daily Devotions for Die-Hard Fans: South Carolina Gamecocks
© 2012 Ed McMinn
Extra Point Publishers; P.O. Box 871; Perry, GA 31069

Library of Congress Cataloging-in-Publication Data
13 ISBN Digit ISBN: 978-0-9882595-7-7

Manufactured in the United States of America.

Visit us at www.die-hardfans.com.

Cover and interior design by Slynn McMinn.

GAMECOCKS

A Note from the Author

This is actually Volume II of *Daily Devotions for Die-Hard Fans: South Carolina Gamecocks*. The devotions and their stories are all new, written for this book. Most of the devotions center on the 2010 and 2011 baseball national championships, the 2012 runners-up, the 2010 football championship of the SEC's East Division, and the record-setting 11-win season of 2011.

As with the first volume (which is still available), my hope is that you enjoy this humble offering, dedicated to the greater glory of God; my prayer is that it in some way proves beneficial to you in your faith life.

-- Ed McMinn

The following titles are available:

DAY 1

PRAYER WARRIORS

Read Luke 18:1-8.

"Then Jesus told his disciples a parable to show them that they should always pray and not give up" (v. 1).

The Gamecocks had something extra going for them in their win over Virginia in the 2011 College World Series: the power of Charlie Peters' prayers.

In April 2003, 5-year-old Charlie was diagnosed with cancer. While he was in an Omaha hospital hooked up to some tubes, a group of college boys in town for the College World Series stopped by his room for a visit. They played some make-believe baseball in the lobby without a ball with Charlie taking a home-run cut and rounding the bases. They were South Carolina Gamecocks.

Head coach Ray Tanner asked Charlie if he'd like to come to the stadium the next day and be the Gamecocks' honorary bat boy. Charlie made a poster for the USC dugout that said, "Never give up." In November, Charlie was declared free of cancer.

When USC returned to Omaha in 2010, Charlie, now 12, missed the first game and the Gamecocks lost. "Where's my Charlie?" Tanner asked. He and his family were there for the next six games as the Gamecocks streaked to the title. He was on the field for the celebration of the championship.

In 2011, Charlie was in the dugout in Omaha, one of the team's two bat boys. Several times during the 3-2, 13-inning win over Virginia (See Devotion No. 42.), Charlie's vision turned skyward.

GAMECOCKS

His parents had taught him to pray, and he decided the team needed a little extra help. Once, Tanner asked him what he was praying for. "A double play," Charlie replied. His prayers for double plays were answered as was his prayer for a run.

The Gamecocks went on to win the national title, setting a College World Series record for consecutive wins, thanks in part to their special bat boy and his prayers.

Charlie Peters prayed and didn't give up. That's exactly what Jesus taught us to do as his followers: always pray and never give up. Any problems we may have with prayer and its results derive from our side, not God's. We pray for a while about something – perhaps fervently at first – but our enthusiasm wanes if we don't receive the answer we want exactly when we want it. Why waste our time by asking for the same thing over and over again?

But God isn't deaf; God does hear our prayers, and God does respond to them. As Jesus clearly taught, our prayers have an impact because they turn the power of Almighty God loose in this world. Thus, falling to our knees and praying to God is not a sign of weakness and helplessness. Rather, praying for someone or something is an aggressive act, an intentional ministry, a conscious and fervent attempt on our part to change someone's life or the world for the better.

God responds to our prayers; we often just can't perceive how he is working to make those prayers come about.

Once we'd get out of a jam, everyone would say, 'Charlie, you've got to get us some runs.'
-- *Charlie Peters on the 3-2 win over Virginia*

Jesus taught us to always pray and never give up.

DAY 2

SUPERSTITION

Read Isaiah 2:6-16.

"They are full of superstitions from the East; . . . they bow down to the work of their hands" (vv. 6b, 8b).

The Gamecock baseball players of 2010 may not have been any more superstitious than other teams -- but then there's the Avatar Spirit Stick.

In USC's opening game of the NCAA Tournament, the boys from Columbia were in trouble against Bucknell, of which it was said, the Bisons "might be the worst team in the entire sixty-four-team field." Bucknell led 5-1 in the sixth inning when junior outfielder Robert Beary decided something had to be done. What he did was in keeping with sophomore pitcher Michael Roth's assertion that the players said and did "stupid stuff all the time."

Beary grabbed a bat, a baseball, and a roll of tape and attached the ball to the bat. He then "galloped around the dugout, yapping at every player to touch the bat." The imagery was simple: Put the bat on the ball. "It should look like this," Beary repeated.

The team broke into laughter, and the whole mood changed. Beary and senior Jeff Jones dubbed the device the "Avatar Spirit Stick," after the blockbuster science fiction movie. They had un-knowingly given birth to the Gamecocks' postseason mascot, one "the team would come to fully believe was enchanted."

The duo began playing with the stick's power, pointing it in various directions. To everyone's amazement, the ball repeatedly

GAMECOCKS

seemed to obey the stick's holder. They pointed the bat to the night sky, for instance, and little-used freshman outfielder Evan Marzilli promptly launched a two-run homer. "We looked at each other like, 'No way,'" Beary said about the stick.

USC rallied for a 9-5 win, and the stick's reputation was born. With the charm along for the ride all the way, the team won eleven of twelve postseason games -- and the national championship.

Superstitions – such as those of the Avatar Spirit Stick – can be benign. Nothing in the Bible warns us about the dangers inherent in walking under ladders or waving a bat and ball around.

God is quite concerned, however, about superstition of a more serious nature such as using the occult to predict the future. Its danger for us is that we allow something other than God to take precedence in our lives; we in effect worship idols.

While most of us scoff at palm readers and psychics, we nevertheless risk being idol worshippers of a different sort. Just watch the frenzied reaction of fans when a movie star or a star football player shows up. Or consider how we often compromise what we know is right merely to save face or to gain favor in the workplace.

Superstition is the stuff of nonsense. Idol worshipping, however, is as real for us today as it was for the Israelites. It is also just as dangerous.

It's pretty dumb when you think about it, but it brought the team together, so maybe it wasn't that dumb at all.
-- Robert Beary on the Avatar Spirit Stick

Superstition in the form of idol worship is alive and well today, occurring anytime we venerate anything other than God.

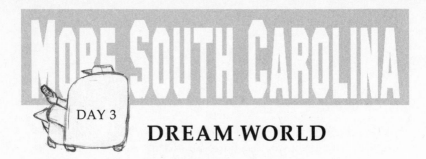

DAY 3

DREAM WORLD

Read Joshua 3.

"All Israel passed by until the whole nation had completed the crossing on dry ground" (v. 17b).

Playing football for South Carolina wasn't a dream come true for Alshon Jeffery at first. It just turned out that way.

After his junior season of 2011, Jeffery traded in his amateur status for the NFL. In his three years as a Gamecock, though, he rewrote the school's record book for wide receivers.

Jeffery's unofficial coming-out party came against Kentucky in 2009 when he caught seven passes for 138 yards and three touchdowns. He was on his way to becoming a freshman All-America. As the Gamecocks claimed the East Division title in 2010, Jeffery was All-America and All-SEC. He set the school season records for receptions (88) and yards (1,517).

After another All-SEC year in the Gamecocks' 11-win season in 2011, Jeffery finished with the school record for career receiving yards (3,042) and tied with Sidney Rice for the USC records for career receiving touchdowns (23) and career 100-yard games (11).

Jeffery's time in Columbia was thus a dream come true. For most of his life, though, being a Gamecock wasn't his dream. In fact, he didn't even dream about playing football. He was committed to basketball and went out for football as a sophomore only after doing the math. At 6'3", he knew he "was the perfect size for a wide receiver. I thought I had a better shot with football."

GAMECOCKS

He was right. Then his dream was to play for USC -- but not the one in Columbia. Jeffery even committed to that school out west before Steve Spurrier had a serious discussion with him about how big a star he would be as a Gamecock. It didn't hurt that his dad refused to fly and his mama had no interest in looking after her boy from across the country.

So Alshon Jeffery made his dreams come true in Columbia -- and helped the whole program realize some of its dreams.

No matter how tightly or doggedly we cling to our dreams, devotion to them won't make them a reality. Moreover, the cold truth is that all too often dreams don't come true even when we put forth a mighty effort. The realization of dreams generally results from a head-on collision of persistence and timing.

But what if our dreams don't come true because they're not the same dreams God has for us? That is, they're not good enough and, in many cases, they're not big enough.

God calls us to great achievements because God's dreams for us are greater than our dreams for ourselves. Could the Israelites, wallowing in the misery of slavery, even dream of a land of their own? Could they imagine actually going to such a place?

The fulfillment of such great dreams occurs only when our dreams and God's will for our lives are the same. Our dreams should be worthy of our best – and worthy of God's involvement in making them come true.

That was my dream school. I thought, one day, I want to go there.
-- Alshon Jeffery on USC (the one in California)

**If our dreams are to come true, they must
be worthy of God's involvement in them.**

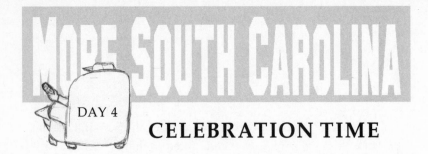
DAY 4

CELEBRATION TIME

Read Luke 15:1-10.

"There is rejoicing in the presence of the angels of God over one sinner who repents" (v. 10).

And so, in Gainesville of all places, the celebration began.

On Nov. 13, 2010, in what was called "arguably the biggest and most significant [win] in program history," the 22nd-ranked USC Gamecocks won in The Swamp for the first-time ever, demolishing the 24th-ranked Florida Gators 36-14. The victory clinched the championship of the SEC East and earned South Carolina a spot in the SEC title game for the first time.

With the win, USC fans celebrated the school's second championship since it began playing football in 1892. The first title belonged to the 1969 team that won the ACC. The victory also finished off the East Division trifecta: It was the first time the Gamecocks had ever beaten the Gators, Tennessee, and Georgia in the same season (a feat duplicated by the 11-win team of 2011).

"It was a good night for South Carolina and the Gamecocks," crowed head coach Steve Spurrier. School president Harris Pastides agreed, declaring the win was "for all the ages, for the fans who have been long suffering and really wanted a championship."

For a heartbreaking moment, it looked as though that long suffering would continue. The Gators returned the opening kickoff 99 yards and led 7-0 only 14 seconds into the game. So thorough, however, was USC's dominance from then on that Florida would not threaten to score again until the game's outcome had been decided in Carolina's favor.

The unruffled Gamecocks went ahead 9-7 for good on a 7-yard run by Marcus Lattimore with 2:37 to play in the first quarter. Lattimore rushed for 212 yards on a school-record forty carries. The helpless Florida offense managed only 67 yards and three first downs through the first three quarters.

"This is one the fans will never forget -- ever," Pastides said as those fans did indeed celebrate.

USC just whipped Clemson. You got that new job or that promotion. You just held your newborn child in your arms. Life has those grand moments that call for celebration. You may jump up and down and scream in a wild frenzy or share a quiet, sedate candlelight dinner at home -- but you celebrate.

Consider then a celebration beyond our imagining, one that fills every corner of the very home of God and the angels. Imagine a celebration in Heaven, which also has its grand moments.

Those grand moments are touched off when someone comes to faith in Jesus. Heaven itself rings with the joyous sounds of the singing and dancing of the celebrating angels. Even God rejoices when just one person – you or someone you have introduced to Christ? -- turns to him.

When you said "yes" to Christ, you made the angels dance.

This is for South Carolina.
-- Steve Spurrier, celebrating the 2010 win over his alma mater

God himself joins the angels in heavenly celebration when even a single person turns to him through faith in Jesus.

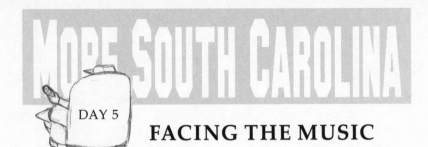
DAY 5

FACING THE MUSIC

Read Psalm 98.

"Sing to the Lord a new song, for he has done marvelous things" (v. 1).

Freshman outfielder Evan Marzilli played on Senior Night 2010. But for him that evening, playing involved more than baseball.

Marzilli moved into the starting lineup during the postseason run of 2010 and was sensational. He was the leading hitter for the national champs in postseason play and was named to the All-Tournament Team in Omaha. As a sophomore, he hit .291 for the 2011 champions. For the runners-up in 2012, he started all 69 games in center field and hit .284 and again was named to the All-Tournament Team in Omaha. After the season, he was drafted by the Arizona Diamondbacks.

As a freshman, Marzilli naturally wasn't honored on May 21, 2010, on Senior Night, but he nevertheless was a big part of the pre-game ceremonies. He pulled out his electric guitar and played the National Anthem. Marzilli's performance became a YouTube sensation among Gamecock fans as he finished off "with a quick flourish that would have made Jimi Hendrix proud."

"The biggest thing is I didn't want to mess up," the freshman confessed. "That was the most nervous I've ever been for anything in my life." He helped ease his nerves by practicing more than 100 times to get the song down.

Marzilli taught himself the guitar in high school, forming a

GAMECOCKS

band and playing bass with some buddies. His move to USC from Rhode Island ended his days in a band, but he didn't lose touch with his guitar. In addition to Senior Night, he often cranked up his amp for his baseball-playing roommates, Christian Walker, Tyler Webb, and Brison Celek. "We had some people last year kind of complain about the noise," Marzilli said.

Nobody complained on Senior Night, but the sweetest music Evan Marzilli made in Columbia was during the games.

Maybe you can't play a lick or carry a tune in the proverbial bucket. Or perhaps you do know your way around a guitar or a keyboard and can hum, whistle, or play "2001" on karaoke night without closing the joint down as people flee for the exits.

Unless you're a professional musician, however, how well you play or sing really doesn't matter. What counts is that you have music in your heart and sometimes you have to turn it loose.

Worshipping God has always included music in some form. That same boisterous and musical enthusiasm you exhibit when the USC Marching Band cranks up at a Gamecock game should be a part of the joy you have in your personal worship of God.

Take a moment to count the blessings in your life, all gifts from God. Then consider that God loves you, he always will, and he has arranged through Jesus for you to spend eternity with him. How can that song God put in your heart not burst forth?

I'm not game for that. There's a difference between 8,000 people and 80,000.
-- Evan Marzilli on playing the National Anthem at a football game

**You call it music; others may call it noise;
sent God's way, it's called praise.**

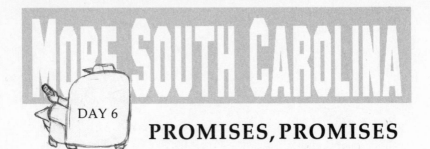

DAY 6

PROMISES, PROMISES

Read 2 Corinthians 1:16-20.

"No matter how many promises God has made, they are 'Yes' in Christ" (v. 20).

When his team was accused of cheating, Gamecock head coach Ray Tanner made his players a promise -- and he kept it.

Prior to the 2011 season, the NCAA mandated changes in the composition of the bats to make them act more like wood bats. The expectation was that the change would reduce home runs.

Apparently the Gamecocks never got the memo. In a 6-3 win over fourth-ranked Clemson on March 4, they slammed three homers. After the Saturday game was rained out, the two teams met Sunday. Jackie Bradley, Jr., led off the game with his third home run of the season. That's when a ruckus started.

The Tiger head coach asked the home plate umpire to check Bradley's bat. It seemed that a Clemson player had picked it up and found that it was hot. "Our bats were in the sun," a puzzled Michael Roth commented. "We were told to move them out of the sun. We were like, 'Is he serious? Is this guy joking?'"

He wasn't; the Clemson coach had accused the Gamecocks of cheating by heating up their bats. Coaches and players alike were incensed, though the home run stood. Tanner said it was the only time in his career he had been accused of cheating.

The rancor increased with players taking to Twitter to vent. Before the Tuesday game, Tanner called a team meeting and

GAMECOCKS

promised the players he would do something he perhaps had never done before: He would publicly make his feelings known if they won. "The players roared. It was a deal."

They won 5-4 and Tanner kept his promise. In the postgame media session, he bluntly stated that he was offended by what had been done to and said about his team. "I don't cheat," he declared. "I just don't think what happened is appropriate," he said, putting the focus on Clemson's offensive actions.

Like Ray Tanner, the promises you make don't say much about you; the promises you keep tell everything.

The promise you made to your daughter to be there for her softball game. To your son to help him with his math homework. To your parents to come see them soon. To your spouse to remain faithful until death. And remember what you promised God?

You may carelessly throw promises around, but you can never outpromise God, who is downright profligate with his promises. For instance, he has promised to love you always, to forgive you no matter what you do, and to prepare a place for you with him in Heaven.

And there's more good news in that God operates on this very simple premise: Promises made are promises kept. You can rely absolutely on God's promises. The people to whom you make them should be able to rely just as surely on your promises.

The players might have been happier about Tanner's uncharacteristic outburst than the win itself.
-- Travis Haney in Gamecock Encore

**God keeps his promises just as those
who rely on you expect you to keep yours.**

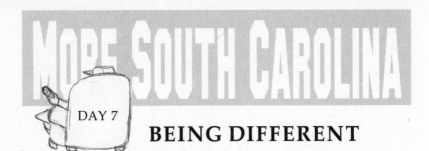

DAY 7

BEING DIFFERENT

Read Daniel 3.

*"We want you to know, O king, that we will not serve
your gods or worship the image of gold you have set up"
(v. 18).*

Life as a high school football player was a little different than
most for Connor Shaw: His head coach was his dad.

Shaw enrolled early at USC after graduating from high school
in December 2009. The head start helped as by the time the 2010
season started, he was second on the depth chart behind Stephen
Garcia. He played in nine games for the SEC East Division champions. By season's end, Shaw was the starter for the 11-win team of
2011. He became only the third quarterback since 1971 to win his
first four starts, joining Steve Taneyhill (1992) and Chris Smelley
(2007). After two seasons, his career completion percentage of 66.1
was the highest in Gamecock history.

Head coach Steve Spurrier's reputation for being tough on his
quarterbacks didn't bother Shaw a bit. As a family member once
asserted, "Connor is used to being pushed." That family member
knew what he was talking about; he was the one who made Connor's football life different in high school. He was Lee, the head
football coach at Flowery Branch, Ga., and Connor played high
school ball for him. He is also Connor's dad.

"As a family, we don't make excuses," the elder Shaw said. "I
was tough," he admitted, sounding like a coach. "I was really

tough on [Connor]."

The Shaw son apparently thrived on the tough way he was handled in high school. "I think being a coach's son helped me tremendously," he said.

And Lee Shaw found the different relationship he had with one of his high-school players to be truly special, and it wasn't only as a football coach. "As a dad, I am a blessed man," he said.

While we live in a secular society that constantly pressures us to conform to its principles and values, we serve a risen Christ who calls us to be different. Therein lies the great conflict of the Christian life in contemporary America.

But how many of us really consider that even in our secular society we struggle to conform? We are all geeks in a sense. We can never truly conform because we were not created by God to live in such a sin-filled world in the first place. Thus, when Christ calls us to be different by following and espousing Christian beliefs, principles, and practices, he is summoning us to the lifestyle we were born for.

The most important step in being different for Jesus is realizing and admitting what we really are: We are children of God; we are Christians. Only secondarily are we citizens of a secular world. That world both scorns and disdains us for being different; Jesus both praises and loves us for it.

There is a little bit of difference in the coach's kids, because they grow up around football all the time.
-- Steve Spurrier, speaking of Connor Show

The lifestyle Jesus calls us to is different from that of the world, but it is the way we were born to live.

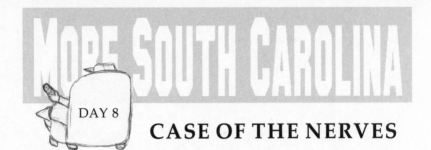

DAY 8

CASE OF THE NERVES

Read Mark 5:1-20.

"What do you want with me, Jesus, Son of the Most High God? Swear to God that you won't torture me!" (v. 7)

One surefire way to get rid of opening-day nerves is to drive in the game-winning run.

As the 2012 baseball season began on Feb. 17 at a packed Carolina Stadium, head coach Ray Tanner had some advice for his newcomers. "You've got a packed house today and you're playing your first game and you want to do well," he said. "You can't let your nerves get into it."

Much easier said than done. In 2011, Peter Mooney broke in at shortstop after transferring from a community college where he played most of his games "in front of crowds that consisted primarily of family and friends." "I was glancing around, thinking this is real life," he said before the first home game of the season in front of more than 8,000 fans. "It was nerve-wracking." Mooney settled down quite well; he hit .280 for the national champs.

In 2012, the first-timers included LB Dantzler at third base, Joey Pankake at shortstop, and Chase Vergason at second base. In all, Tanner started four freshman and two junior-college transfers.

Dantzler had expected that playing before a full house of rabid Gamecock fans would be a whole new ball game for him. After all, he had previously played his college ball at a school "that has more letters in its name than it has baseball fans in its stands."

GAMECOCKS

The VMI Keydets provided some tough opening-day competition. With the score 1-1, Dantzler came to the plate with two outs in the bottom of the eighth and Evan Marzilli at second. He lined a single to center on a 0-2 count to score Marzilli. The 2-1 final was on the board.

Standing at first, Dantzler said after the game, "was pretty cool" as he looked around and saw "everybody going crazy." So much for a case of the nerves.

We often can't really explain why some situations make us nervous. Making a speech, for instance. Or being in the presence of a person we'd like to ask out.

We probably rarely if ever consider the possibility that we make other people nervous. Who in the world could be intimidated by us? Try this on for starters: Satan himself. Yep, that very demon of darkness that Hollywood repeatedly portrays as so powerful that goodness is helpless before him. That's the one.

But we can make Satan nervous only if we stand before him with the power of Jesus Christ at our disposal. As Christians, we seem to understand that our basic mission is to further Jesus' kingdom and to change the world through emulating him in the way we live and love others. But do we appreciate that in truly living for Jesus, we are daily tormenting the very devil himself?

Satan and his lackeys quake helplessly in fear and nervousness before the power of almighty God that is in us through Jesus.

I had the butterflies and I've been doing it for a long time.
-- Ray Tanner on opening day 2012

Nervous and apprehensive -- so stands Satan himself in the presence of a follower of Jesus.

TRAGEDY

Read Job 1, 2:1-10.

"In all this, Job did not sin by charging God with wrongdoing" (v. 1:22).

Each spring a memorial award is presented to a football player not to remember a USC legend but as a reminder of the school's greatest athletic tragedy.

During every spring football game, the Steve Sisk Memorial Award is presented to the team's best blocker from the season before. The players and the fans can certainly be forgiven if they don't have a clue who Steve Sisk is. After all, he never played a down for the Gamecocks.

Sisk "was a fullback at A.C. Flora [in Columbia] in a defensive tackle's body." Despite his size (6-foot-2, 245 lbs.), Sisk rarely ran the ball. Instead, he was a blocker who terrorized opposing linebackers and defensive backs.

Deciding on a college was never an issue for Sisk. A South Carolina assistant coach was at practically every one of A.C. Flora's practices in 1968. When Sisk left home for his first day of practice in August 1969, he told his parents he was on his way to be "the best football player South Carolina has ever had."

On Sept. 4, a sweltering Wednesday, the Gamecocks practiced as usual. That evening, the family's dinner was interrupted by a phone call with tragic news. Sisk had collapsed on the practice field and had been rushed unconscious to a hospital. Kidney complications developed, and he died on Monday, Sept. 8, the only football player in USC history to in effect die on the athletic field. He was 18 years old.

As Sisk's name gradually faded into obscurity, the USC Letterman's Club in 1999 began presenting the award as a memorial to remember a Gamecock who gave his life for the program.

While we may be hit by them in varying degrees, suffering and tragedy are par for life's course. What we do with tragedy when it strikes us determines to a great extent how we live the rest of our lives.

We can – in accordance with the bitter suggestion Job's wife offered -- "Curse God and die," or we can trust God and live. That is, we can plunge into endless despair or we can lean upon the power of a transcendent faith in an almighty God who offers us hope in our darkest hours.

We don't have to understand tragedy; we certainly don't have to like it or believe there's anything fair about it as was the case with Steve Sisk's death. What we must do in such times, however, is trust in God's all-powerful love for us and his promise that all things will work for good for those who love him.

In choosing a life of ongoing trust in God in the face of our suffering, we prevent the greatest tragedy of all: that of a soul being cast into Hell.

I've had a lot of people die in my life. If I could bring one of them back, it would be Steve [Sisk].

-- Joe Sligh, a friend

Tragedy can drive us into despair and death or into the life-sustaining arms of almighty God.

CHANGELESS

Read Hebrews 13:5-16.

"Jesus Christ is the same yesterday and today and forever" (v. 8).

Frustrated by the collapse of his bullpen in the 2009 regional, USC pitching coach Mark Calvi decided it was time for a change.

Calvi served as Ray Tanner's pitching coach for six seasons, leaving after the 2010 season to take over the program at South Alabama. As the team's postseason losses and disappointments mounted over the years, Calvi's thinking gradually changed. He had leaned heavily on the various aces of his staffs. For instance, his first staff in 2005 basically had only two starters: Aaron Rawl and Zac McCamie. He also had a capable closer in Brent Marsh. After that, what happened was pretty much anybody's guess.

Calvi realized that each season something was missing in his staff, whether it were starters, a closer, or middle relievers. Thus, to win games, he wound up using his most reliable pitchers all season, "taxing them to the point of breakdown by the postseason."

Calvi's frustration reached its boiling point after the loss at East Carolina in the 2009 regional finals. His exhausted staff couldn't hold a three-run lead in the ninth inning. Back in Columbia, the assistant boldly strode into his boss's office and told him things were about to change.

Calvi wanted to use more pitchers in a game; that meant, of course, using more pitchers all season long. He wanted to manage his staff as major-league managers did -- forcing match-ups that favored the pitcher -- instead of using the same pitchers over and over again.

It worked. Rather than tiring out in the postseason as they had in the past, the Gamecock pitchers posted a 2.15 ERA at the 2010 College World Series, more than a point lower than any other team. And what the team did there is, of course, Carolina legend.

Laptops and smart phones, high definition TVs, and cars that park themselves – much that is common in your life now wasn't even around when you were 16. Think about how style, music, and tax laws constantly change. As Mark Calvi's approach shows, even a staid old game such as baseball changes sometimes.

You shouldn't be too harsh on this old world, though, because you've changed also. You've aged, gained or lost weight, gotten married, changed jobs, or relocated.

Change in our contemporary times is often so rapid that it is bewildering and confusing, leaving us casting about for something to hold on to that will always be the same, that we can use as an anchor for our lives. Is there anything in this world like that; is there anything that is impervious to change?

Sadly, the answer's no. All the things of this world change.

On the other hand, there's Jesus, who is the same today and the same forever, always dependable, always loving you. No matter what happens in our lives, Jesus is still the same.

If you've got them, use them. What are you waiting for?
-- Ray Tanner to Mark Calvi on the change in pitching philosophy

Jesus is the same forever;
his love for you will never change.

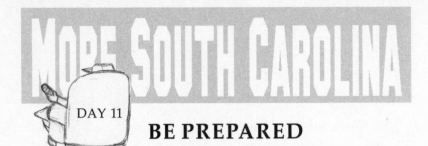
DAY 11

BE PREPARED

Read Matthew 10:5-23.

"I am sending you out like sheep among wolves. Therefore be as shrewd as snakes and as innocent as doves" (v. 16).

When Marcus Lattimore went down, the Gamecock season didn't because freshman Brandon Wilds was prepared to step up.

Lattimore exploded onto the national scene in 2010 as a true freshman running back. His 1,197 yards rushing was the third-best total in Gamecock history behind George Rogers' totals in 1979 and 1980. He was a unanimous choice as the SEC Freshman of the Year and the National Freshman of the Year.

Lattimore was on his way to a sensational sophomore season in 2011 with 818 yards rushing in seven games when he suffered a season-ending knee injury. The blow appeared to be a devastating one to the USC season. As one writer put it, the injury "left many questioning whether South Carolina could salvage its running game over the remainder of the year."

The question was a legitimate one because the Gamecocks didn't have a wealth of experience in reserve. The best they could come up with was a little-used freshman named Brandon Wilds. He had started the season fifth on the depth chart, but injuries to the four backs ahead of him left him as the last man standing.

It turned out, though, that Wilds was ready to be an SEC-caliber running back. He made his debut as a starter against Tennessee and a hostile crowd and rushed for 137 yards on 28 carries in the

14-3 win. He was also the leading receiver with 31 yards.

Wilds was among the very few who weren't surprised by his play because he felt he was prepared for the job. "I worked hard all throughout the summer," he said. "I expected to get 100."

"He's a good back," affirmed head coach Steve Spurrier.

Wilds was ready all season long, rushing for 486 yards on 4.5 yards per carry for the record-setting 11-2 Gamecocks.

Like Brandon Wilds, you know the importance of preparation in your own life. You went to the bank for a car loan, facts and figures in hand. That presentation you made at work was seamless because you practiced. The kids' school play suffered no meltdowns because they rehearsed. Knowing what you need to do and doing what you must to succeed isn't luck; it's preparation.

Jesus understood this, and he prepared his followers by lecturing them and by sending them out on field trips. Two thousand years later, the life of faith requires similar training and study. You prepare so you'll be ready when that unsaved neighbor standing beside you at your backyard grill asks about Jesus. You prepare so you will know how God wants you to live. You prepare so you are certain in what you believe when the secular, godless world challenges it.

And one day you'll see God face to face. You certainly want to be prepared for that.

I just worked hard.
-- Brandon Wilds on how he prepared himself to play

Living in faith requires constant study
and training, preparation for the day
when you meet God face to face.

DAY 12

QUIET TIME

Read 1 Kings 19:1-13.

"And after the earthquake a fire, but the Lord was not in the fire: and after the fire a still small voice" (v. 12 KJV).

His play on the field did the talking for Devin Taylor. That and his wrist bands.

Young men "don't have to be real talkative to be good players," declared head Gamecock Steve Spurrier. He was referring to Taylor, a defensive end who entered the 2012 season as a senior with the reputation as the football team's quiet man.

Blessed with what has been described as "preposterously long arms," Taylor festooned each arm with wrist bands, four each in fact. They said "more about him that he will say about himself." Two of the bands remembered acquaintances with cancer. Others are symbols and reminders of his Christian faith; others recognize military veterans. "I just like wearing bands," he explained.

For Taylor, that amounted to a conversation because at USC he was well known as a man who spoke sparingly and softly. Offensive lineman Rokevious Watkins counted himself among the fortunate few because Taylor "actually talks to me," he once said. "We actually sit down and have conversations."

There was never anything unassuming about Taylor's play on the field, though. He was first-team All-SEC as a sophomore and honorable mention All-SEC in 2011. In the USC record book, he is among the leaders all-time in sacks and tackles for loss.

GAMECOCKS

Taylor came by his quiet nature honestly as his father is a quiet man. He grew up working the register in the front of his dad's restaurant until his head started scraping the low ceiling when he was 16. He had to change jobs and move to the back. "And then he grew three more inches," his dad said.

Chances are, though, Taylor kept quiet about it.

The television blares; the ring tone sounds off; the dishwasher rattles. Outside, the roar of traffic assaults your ears; a siren screams until you wince; the garbage collectors bang and slam the cans around; and everybody shouts to be heard above the din.

Though Devin Taylor may not contribute a lot to the clamor, we live in a noisy world. Strangely enough, the most powerful voice of all – the one whose voice spoke the universe into being -- does not join in the cacophony. We would expect Almighty God to speak in a thunderous roar, complete with lightning, that forces us to cover our ears and fall to our knees in dread.

Instead, God patiently waits for us to turn to him, nudging us gently with a still small voice. Thus, in the serenity of quiet time expressly set aside for God, and not in the daily tumult, do we find God and discover something rather remarkable: that God's being with us is not remarkable at all. He's always there; we just can't hear him most of the time over the world's noise.

It's a lot better to be seen than heard. The sun is the most powerful thing I know of, and it doesn't make much noise.
                                                    -- Bear Bryant

**God speaks in a whisper, not a shout,
so we must listen carefully,
or we will miss his voice altogether.**

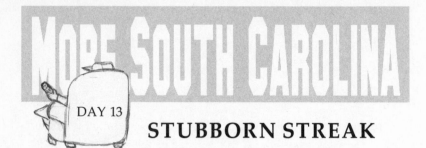

DAY 13

STUBBORN STREAK

Read Ephesians 6:10-20.

*"Stand firm then, with the belt of truth buckled around
your waist" (v. 14).*

The doctors told Jackie Bradley, Jr., his college baseball career
was over, but they had no idea how stubborn he was.

The MVP of the 2010 College World Series and one of the best
defensive outfielders in the history of the collegiate game, Bradley
injured his left wrist in a game against Mississippi State on April
23, 2011. He attempted a diving catch but slipped on the damp
grass and landed awkwardly on his wrist.

The ball was jarred from his glove, and Bradley instinctively
retrieved it. When he squared himself up to throw, he felt his
wrist pop out of place. He lobbed the ball into the infield, reset
the wrist in place, and finished the half-inning. In the dugout, he
tried to swing a bat. "It was the worst pain I'd ever felt," he said.
He was done for the day.

In Columbia, Bradley learned he was done for more than just
a day or two. He had a slight tear of the cartilage in his wrist that
would require surgery. He would be sidelined for ten to twelve
weeks. With the College World Series cranking up seven weeks
after his surgery, the implication was clear: Bradley was through.

He didn't buy it. He told his teammates, "Make it to Omaha
and I'll be back." He stubbornly locked his mind onto the idea
that there was no way to keep him from playing.

GAMECOCKS

On June 14, two days before the team was to leave for Omaha, Bradley was cleared by his doctors to play. He looked good during his first batting practice. "I think we're going to have to put him [in] there," head coach Ray Tanner said. Just past the eighth week after his injury, Bradley started the first game of the College World Series.

Stubbornness is not necessarily a virtue. Most of us have run across people who are "pigheaded." That is, they won't listen to reason, they won't change their mind, they won't do what everyone else knows they should. They're just stubborn for no other reason than that's the way they are.

Stubbornness can be exactly what a situation demands, however, as Jackie Bradley, Jr.'s stubbornness in the face of his doctors' expectations demonstrates. We should be stubborn when we know the truth and are called upon to defend it. In no other aspect of our lives is stubbornness more necessary than in our faith.

That's because in Jesus, we know truth. It's not the truth that we vehemently espouse only as long as it is convenient or serves our purposes; that "truth" is what passes for truth in the world. Rather, in Jesus we know absolute truth.

That truth – the soul-saving message of the Gospel – is under attack today, which is nothing new. Just as he always has, Jesus needs stubborn Christians, those who know his truth, live it, and share it with others no matter what they say.

We thought that was it, yeah. We thought his career was over.
-- USC assistant coach Chad Holbrook on Jackie Bradley, Jr.'s injury

To follow Jesus is to be unceasingly and relentlessly stubborn for him.

DAY 14

THE HOMEPLACE

Read Joshua 24:14-27.

*"Choose for yourselves this day whom you will serve. . . .
But as for me and my household, we will serve the Lord"
(v. 15).*

On Feb. 21, 2009, head baseball coach Ray Tanner and his boys officially moved into their new home. Fittingly, they celebrated moving day with a win.

For a decade, Tanner dreamed of and fought for a new baseball facility for his Gamecocks. He fully understood the decades-long history of success the program had enjoyed in Sarge Frye Field, which opened in 1977. On May 11, 1980, the facility was officially named for a longtime grounds keeper.

Sarge Frye Field was described as "lovable" and "historically charming." As the record shows, the Gamecocks over the years consistently vied for the SEC title and a berth in the College World Series. Tanner, however, was convinced that the program could do more with "a newer, bigger and brighter park." USC could move up. "They could go from very good to great" with a park that would allow Tanner and his staff to recruit the very best players and that would heighten enthusiasm among USC fans.

So Tanner went to work. As writer Travis Haney put it, the coach's "calves were in excellent shape from all the hoop-jumping that came along with a political process that required years of patience and posturing."

GAMECOCKS

But Tanner got his stadium. The 2009 season opened with the christening of Carolina Stadium. Darius Rucker sang the national anthem. Former USC coaches June Raines and Bobby Richardson helped Tanner cut the ribbon that officially opened the park.

The Gamecocks beat Duquesne 13-0 that day and thus began what immediately became a habit of winning at home. Through the 2012 season, USC was 124-26 in the new digs, a remarkable winning percentage of .827.

Like the Gamecocks at a game in Carolina Stadium, you enter your home to find love, security, and joy. It's the place where your heart feels warmest, your laughter comes easiest, and your life is its richest. It is the center of and the reason for everything you do and everything you are.

How can a home be such a place?

If it is a home where grace is spoken before every meal, it is such a place. If it is a home where the Bible is read, studied, and discussed by the whole family gathered together, it is such a place. If it is a home that serves as a jumping-off point for the whole family to go to church, not just on Sunday morning and not just occasionally, but regularly, it is such a place. If it is a home where the name of God is spoken with reverence and awe and not with disrespect and indifference, it is such a place.

In other words, a house becomes a true home when God is part of the family.

The best collegiate only baseball park in the nation.
-- Design firm's Ryan Sickman on Carolina Stadium

A home is full when all the family members --
including God -- are present.

DAY 15

THE GAME OF LIFE

Read 1 Corinthians 9:24-27.

Run in such a way as to get the prize (v. 24b).

Tori Gurley bought a ticket to a football game, and that started him on the way to putting his life together.

From Rock Hill, Gurley failed to qualify academically out of high school after starring in both football and basketball. With nothing else to do, he moved in with his grandmother in Birmingham and took a job with a home improvement company. "I went from being an all-state caliber guy to a guy who was working 9-to-5 and taking care of my grandmother," he recalled.

Suffering from heart troubles, Gurley's grandmother needed his help, and he didn't mind the work. Instead, the low point in his young life came the day he scalped a ticket to a University of Alabama-Birmingham football game. "That was the first time in my life I bought a ticket to a football game," he said. Sitting in the stands made him hungry to play football again and to give his life some direction and purpose.

He got a chance when a coach from a New Hampshire prep school spotted him in a pickup basketball game. Gurley not only played basketball and football, but he applied himself academically. In fact, he did so well with the books that the NCAA didn't believe it. He improved so much on his SAT scores that the NCAA was suspicious and made him take the test again.

When his test scores were approved, Gurley came back home

GAMECOCKS

and joined the Gamecocks in 2008. As a redshirt freshman in 2009, he started five games and was fourth on the team with 31 catches and a pair of touchdowns. He was the second leading receiver behind Alshon Jeffery for the 2010 East Division champs. Against Vanderbilt that season, he tied a school record with 14 catches.

"It's an incredible story," said one of the prep school coaches about Gurley's life, which took yet another turn when he signed with the Green Bay Packers in 2011.

Like football, life may be thought of as a game, but where are the rules? Who sets them or does everybody play by his or her own rules? What is the object of the game? How do we win, since every life ends in the same way – with death – and there's really no set time when or specified manner for how that end occurs?

If life is a game, it's a chaotic one that really doesn't make any sense at all. Unless the game is played according to the rules set up the master gamer of them all, Almighty God. His rules are spelled out quite clearly in his instruction book. The game according to God has a clearly defined object: to glorify Him.

Most importantly, the life as played God's way has clearly defined winners and losers. The winners are those who seek out God and find their salvation in Jesus Christ. And the prize for winning is the greatest grand prize of them all: eternal life in Heaven.

Play ball.

Hey, I need to get my life together.
                              -- Tori Gurley at a UAB football game

**Life played God's way is the most exciting
and rewarding game of them all.**

DAY 16

GOOD NEWS

Read Matthew 28:1-10.

'"He has risen from the dead and is going ahead of you into Galilee. There you will see him.' Now I have told you" (v. 7).

Marty Markett was busy trying to cobble together a financial aid package so he could stay in school and on the football team when he got some good news that solved the problem.

Markett came to USC in 2008 on a track scholarship. He was an All-American in the 4x100 relay. In August of 2009, he decided to walk on to the football team. He hadn't played football for a while, but the coaches were quickly smitten with his speed and his intelligence. Not surprisingly, considering his track background, Markett was the fastest player on the squad. He earned a spot on the roster but broke his arm and missed the whole 2009 season.

In 2010, Markett saw his first action as a special teams player. He was so good in the 38-24 win over Tennessee that he earned a game ball from the coaches and a spot in the defensive back rotation. On Nov. 13, Markett truly arrived when he started against Florida in the game that clinched the division title.

But that success didn't earn him a scholarship, so on August 20, 2011, he was in the financial aid office looking for a student loan. When he realized he was going to be late for a team meeting, he texted fellow defensive backs Akeem Auguste and C.C. Whitlock and asked them to let the coaches know. The pair responded with

GAMECOCKS

some really good news: Markett would be going on scholarship.

He left the financial aid office and headed for practice. Sure enough, when he arrived, head coach Steve Spurrier pulled him aside and delivered the news himself: Markett had earned the squad's 85th and final scholarship.

He became a starter in the fifth game of the season, finishing with 26 tackles and using his speed to provide tight coverage and thus shut down some of the league's premier receivers.

The story of mankind's "progress" through the millennia could be summarized and illustrated quite well in an account of how we disseminate our news. For much of recorded history, we told our stories through word of mouth, which required time to spread across political and geographical boundaries. That method also didn't do much to ensure accuracy.

Today, though, our news is instantaneous as Marty Markett's was through the texts from teammates. Yesterday's news is old news; we want to see it and hear about it as it happens.

But the biggest news story in the history of the world goes virtually unnoticed every day by the so-called mainstream media. It is, in fact, often treated as nothing more than superstition. But it's true, and it is the greatest, most wonderful news of all.

What headline should be blaring from every news source in the world? This one: "Jesus Rises from Dead, Defeats Death." It's still today's news, and it's still the most important news story ever.

To receive that scholarship helps out a lot.
-- Marty Markett after he got the good news

The biggest news story in history took place when Jesus Christ walked out of that tomb.

MORE SOUTH CAROLINA

DAY 17

MAKE NO MISTAKE

Read Mark 14:66-72.

"Then Peter remembered the word Jesus had spoken to him: 'Before the rooster crows twice you will disown me three times.' And he broke down and wept" (v. 72).

One of the most exciting and glorious moments in South Carolina sports history included a mistake that had it been spotted would have wiped it all out.

The 2010 Gamecock baseball team rebounded from a 4-3 loss to Oklahoma in the opening game of the College World Series to blast and eliminate top-ranked Arizona State 11-4. For their troubles, they got Oklahoma again with the loser going home.

The Sooners led 1-0 until with one out in the bottom of the seventh, Christian Walker's single chased home Evan Marzilli. That 1-1 score held up until the top of the twelfth when a Sooner home run put the Gamecocks' collective backs against the wall.

Robert Beary kept hope alive with a lead-off single and then stole second with one out. A popup, though, left Beary sitting at second. The Gamecocks were down to their last out.

That out belonged to center fielder Jackie Bradley, Jr., the team's best hitter that season. He was riding an eighteen-game hitting streak, but that night against the Sooners he was 0-for-5. The count went to 2-2, sending USC down to its last strike. After a ball, Bradley ripped the 3-2 pitch into right field to chase Beary home.

Jeff Jones walked, pushing Bradley to second base, and then

GAMECOCKS

designated hitter Brady Thomas drilled a shot off the mound that skipped into center field. The Sooners didn't even try to make a play as Bradley scored easily, sliding into home plate for style points. The celebration of the unlikely win began.

But third-base coach Chad Holbrook knew that Bradley had made a big mistake. He had missed third base on his way home from second. If the Sooners appealed, the run would be negated and the game would continue. But they didn't and it didn't.

It's distressing but it's true: We all make mistakes. Only one perfect man ever walked on this earth, and no one of us is he. Some mistakes are just dumb. Like locking yourself out of your car or falling into a swimming pool with your clothes on.

Other mistakes are more significant and carry with them the potential for devastation. Like heading down a path to addiction. Committing a crime. Walking out on a spouse and the children.

All these mistakes, however, from the momentarily annoying to the life-altering tragic, share one aspect: They can all be forgiven in Christ. Other folks may not forgive us; we may not even forgive ourselves. But God will forgive us when we call upon him in Jesus' name.

Thus, the twofold fatal mistake we can make is ignoring the fact that we will die one day and subsequently ignoring the fact that Jesus is the only way to shun Hell and enter Heaven. We absolutely must get this one right.

If you're not making mistakes, then you're not doing anything.
-- John Wooden

Only one mistake we make sends us to Hell
when we die: ignoring Jesus while we live.

MAKE NO MISTAKE   37

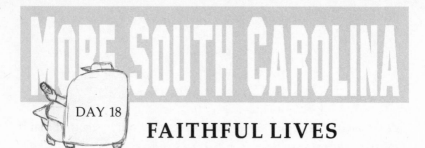

DAY 18

FAITHFUL LIVES

Read Hebrews 11:1-12.

"Faith is the substance of things hoped for, the evidence of things not seen" (v. 1 NKJV).

Steve Spurrier's faith in Lorenzo Ward was immediately rewarded in the 2012 Capital One Bowl -- but it sure didn't look like it at first.

On Dec. 27, 2011, Spurrier gave Ward a late Christmas present, a promotion to the position of full-time defensive coordinator. For six days, Ward had been the interim defensive boss, ever since Ellis Johnson had left to become Southern Miss' head coach. Ward understood the faith his boss was showing in him. "It's a blessing that coach Spurrier feels the way he does about me," Ward said.

His debut came in the Capital One Bowl against Nebraska, which averaged just under 400 yards a game during the season. Ward's preparation continued right on through game day as he stayed up until 5 a.m. studying videos of Nebraska's offense.

Nevertheless, the Cornhuskers scored touchdowns on their first two possessions, not exactly the scintillating start the rookie coordinator had in mind. From then on, though, he demonstrated why Spurrier had so much faith in his ability to lead the defense. Nebraska managed only 253 yards the rest of the game. Most importantly, the Cornhuskers didn't score again.

In the face of the scary start, Ward remained calm. "This team hasn't panicked all season," he said. "We've been behind before."

GAMECOCKS

The defense made some adjustments, but mostly Ward told his players to get more physical, which they did. The defensive front seven had a season-high six sacks, led by Jadeveon Clowney with a pair. Cornerback Stephon Gilmore had an interception that led to a touchdown, and safety D.J. Swearinger forced a fumble to stop a Nebraska drive.

With a new coordinator the head coach had faith in, USC won its history-making 11th game 30-13 "on the backs of its defense."

Your faith forms the heart and soul of what you are. Faith in people, things, ideologies, and concepts to a large extent determines how you spend your life. You believe in the Gamecocks, in your family, in the basic goodness of Americans, in freedom and liberty, and in abiding by the law. These beliefs mold you and make you the person you are.

This is all great stuff, of course, that makes for decent human beings and productive lives. None of it, however, is as important as what you believe about Jesus. To have faith in Jesus is to believe his message of hope and salvation as recorded in the Bible. True faith in Jesus, however, has an additional component; it must also include a personal commitment to him. In other words, you don't just believe in Jesus; you live for him.

Faith in Jesus does more than shape your life; it determines your eternity.

He's the best guy I could hire. That's why I hired him.
-- Steve Spurrier on Lorenzo Ward

Your belief system is the foundation
upon which you build a life; faith in Jesus
is the foundation for your eternal life.

DAY 19

HOPE CHEST

Read Psalm 42.

"Put your hope in God, for I will yet praise him, my Savior and my God" (v. 5b).

Hope was about all the Gamecocks and their fans had going for them as they took on Clemson in 1941 -- but it was enough.

On Big Thursday 1941, the Carolina campus was covered with signs from the students, clear indications that this particular contest was a serious affair in Columbia. In truth, the students and the alums were quite angry. Clemson had beaten the Gamecocks seven years in a row, and they wanted this one badly.

Abe Fennell of *The State* noticed a sense of "renewed hope" for the Gamecocks; Carolina, he said, had "a better chance of winning than in a long time." That really wasn't saying very much. The Tigers were 4-0 and were the defending champions of the Southern Conference; they roared into Big Thursday ranked 14th in the country and 13-point favorites over 1-1-1 USC.

That renewed hope won out. South Carolina jumped out to an 18-0 lead and held on for the 18-14 upset. One columnist wrote, "The Gamecocks outrushed, out passed and all the way around outplayed Clemson who roared out of the hills like its Tiger but trotted back like a lamb."

The State referred to the win as "Rainbow's End." The students got an extra treasure out of it; the excited powers that be cancelled Friday classes. The bell rang on campus all night even when some sleepy soul called the police. They ignored the complaint; "if ever there were a case for allowing a disturbance of peace, this was it."

Head coach Rex Enright got a new Cadillac out of the win. With Clemson moving to the USC 17-yard line on its last possession, one author noted, "The difference between a coffin and a Cadillac is just a few feet of dirt." And a lot of hope.

Only when a life has no hope does it become not worth the living. To hope is not merely to want something; that is desire or wishful thinking. Desire must be coupled with some degree of expectation to produce hope.

Therein lies the great problem. We may wish for a million dollars, relief from our diabetes, world peace, or a way to lose weight while stuffing ourselves with doughnuts and fried chicken. Our hopes, however, must be firmly grounded, or they will inevitably lead us to disappointment, shame, and disaster. In other words, false hopes ruin us.

One of the most basic issues of our lives, therefore, becomes discovering or locating that in which we can place our hope. Where can we find sure promises for a future that we can count on? Where can we place our hope with realistic expectations that we can live securely even though some of the promises we rely on are yet to be delivered?

In God. In God and God alone lies our hope.

Hope springs eternal . . ., and those Carolina supporters will be in there cheering for their favorites and hoping for an upset.
   -- Abe Fennell of The State *on the 1941 USC-Clemson game*

God and his sustaining power are the source of the only meaningful hope possible in our lives.

DAY 20

THE LONG SHOTS

Read Matthew 9:9-13.

"[Jesus] saw a man named Matthew sitting at the tax collector's booth. 'Follow me,' he told him, and Matthew got up and followed him" (v. 9).

While the 2011 national championship may seem obvious in retrospect, the Gamecocks were really long shots to repeat.

Head man Ray Tanner's expectations for the season didn't necessarily include a second title. "The statistics, the percentages of doing that are stacked against you," he said. "The only thing I kept holding onto was, 'Let's have a good team. Let's have a good season. Let's get to the postseason. Let's get a chance to go to a regional.' And then you try to do well when you get there."

The Gamecocks certainly did that. They became the first team in major college history to go 10-0 in an NCAA tournament. They set all-time records by winning sixteen straight tournament games and eleven straight world-series match-ups. They were only the sixth team in NCAA history to win back-to-back titles. That sounds a lot like a powerhouse.

But even the players agreed they were long shots. "We're not the most talented team, and we don't have the best players position for position," assessed junior starting pitcher Michael Roth. "But," he added, "we go out and stick together as a team. We battle. I can't describe it."

The Gamecocks certainly battled in Omaha. Three of their first four wins came in their last at-bat. They worked their way out of bases-loaded situations four times over two games. In Game 1 of the finals against Florida, left fielder Jake Williams threw out what would have been the game-winning run at the plate. (See Devotion No. 47.) First baseman Christian Walker struggled with a broken wrist. (See Devotion No. 23.)

The only time the Gamecocks didn't look like a long shot in Omaha was in the final game when they beat Florida 7-2.

Like the 2011 Gamecocks, Matthew the tax collector was a long shot. In his case, he was an unlikely person to be a confidant of the Son of God. While we may not get all warm and fuzzy about the IRS, our government's revenue agents are nothing like Matthew and his ilk. He bought a franchise, paying the Roman Empire for the privilege of extorting, bullying, and stealing everything he could from his own people. Tax collectors of the time were "despicable, vile, unprincipled scoundrels."

And yet, Jesus said only two words to this lowlife: "Follow me." Jesus knew that this long shot would make an excellent disciple.

It's the same with us. While we may not be quite as vile as Matthew was, none of us can stand before God with our hands clean and our hearts pure. We are all impossibly long shots to enter God's Heaven. That is, until we do what Matthew did: get up and follow Jesus.

We're a bunch of averages Joes [who] come out and battle.
-- Michael Roth on the long-shot champions of 2011

**Only through Jesus does our status change
from being long shots to enter God's Kingdom
to being odds-on favorites.**

DAY 21

GOOD TIMES

Read Psalm 30.

"You turned my wailing into dancing; you removed my
sackcloth and clothed me with joy" (v. 11).

Even when the Gamecocks made a mistake, head coach Ray
Tanner figured something good would happen anyhow. Those
were good times in that 2010 College World Series.

Perhaps not at any moment during the amazing run to the 2010
national championship were times any better than they were in
the first game of the championship series against UCLA. Simply
put, the ball bounced USC's way all night long. Against a Bruin
pitcher who had been drafted in the first round by the Yankees,
the Gamecocks couldn't hit the ball hard early on. Yet, they led
5-0 in the third.

USC scored in the first on a bunt, a bloop, and a check swing.
Another run scored on an error on a routine grounder. The lead
went to 3-0 with another run in the second.

The Gamecocks then loaded the bases with nobody out in the
top of the third. In the dugout, Tanner knew this was the chance
for his team to break the game open. Instead, a fly ball out was
too short to score a run. When the outfielder overthrew home
plate, Scott Wingo tried to score. He was thrown out.

Tanner turned to pitching coach Mark Calvi after that disaster
and said, "That didn't work out very well." "No, it didn't," Calvi
agreed. But Tanner was very aware of the good times his team

GAMECOCKS

was enjoying. "The way we're going," he said, "(Bobby) Haney will drive in those other two." Haney was the no.-8 hitter in the lineup and didn't have an RBI in the series. He promptly singled to drive in both runners. It was 5-0.

Calvi just looked over to his head coach and shook his head. "We were in a position for good things to happen" was the way Tanner explained it after the 7-1 romp. The good times kept coming with the subsequent 2-1 win over UCLA that clinched the title.

Here's a basic but distressing fact about the good times in our lives: They don't last. We may laugh in the sunshine today, but we do so while we symbolically glance over a shoulder. The Gamecocks win today but turn around and lose the next day. We know that sometime – maybe tomorrow – we will cry in the rain as the good times suddenly come crashing down around us.

Awareness of the certainty that good times don't endure often drives many of us to lose our lives and our souls in a lifestyle devoted to the frenetic pursuit of "fun." This is nothing more, though, than a frantic, pitiable, and doomed effort to outrun the bad times lurking around the corner.

The good times will come and go. Only when we quit chasing the good times and instead seek the good life through Jesus Christ do we discover an eternity in which the good times will never end. Only then will we be forever joyous.

You go through times where you just kind of feel like something [good] is going to happen.
– Ray Tanner, speaking of the 2010 College World Series

Let the good times roll – forever and ever
for the followers of Jesus Christ.

DAY 22

PITY PARTY

Read Matthew 16:21-28.

"'Never, Lord!' he said. 'This shall never happen to you!'
Jesus turned and said to Peter, 'Get behind me, Satan!
You are a stumbling block to me'" (vv. 22b-23a).

DeVonte Holloman actually felt sorry for the other team.

Holloman was a starting sophomore safety when USC took on Georgia on Sept. 11, 2010. He also started at safety in 2011; in 2012, he was moved to the key spur spot, which is a hybrid linebacker/safety position.

Holloman racked up seven tackles and forced a fumble in the 17-6 win over Georgia that got the Gamecocks off and running on their way to the SEC East Division title. Thus, he was really rough on the Bulldog offense. That didn't stop him, however, from feeling pity for the Bulldog defense as he stood on the sideline and watched what the Gamecock offense did all night long.

"When you know what's coming, you know who's getting the ball," he said after the game, "it's kind of hard for you defensively when you are not stopping it." "It" was play No. 13, "the Gamecocks' bread-and-butter running play." The "who" Holloman spoke of was freshman tailback Marcus Lattimore. "That's my favorite play," Lattimore said.

With good reason. Even though Georgia knew the play and Lattimore were coming, they couldn't stop him. "Did we run any different plays?" an exuberant Steve Spurrier asked facetiously after the game. "Two tight ends, give the ball to Marcus over left guard and let him go wherever he wanted to."

The key, Spurrier said, was Lattimore's having his shoulder pads square when he hit the line, a technique Lattimore credited running backs coach Jay Graham with developing in him. Given that, Lattimore said, "You can break anybody's tackle; it doesn't matter how big they are."

Which was enough to make even DeVonte Holloman feel a little pity for the Bulldogs.

Pity, even when it involves the plight of a hapless opposing team, is a noble sentiment. Christ displayed it repeatedly, from his encounter with the ten lepers to the tears he wept over the death of his friend Lazarus. To feel true sorrow for the sufferings or misfortune of someone else – to feel pity – is indeed Christlike.

But even pity has its limits, and Jesus defined them when he rebuked Peter, who seemed to say the right thing when he expressed horror at Jesus' declarations of suffering and death. The danger in Peter's attitude was that it urged Jesus to feel sorry for himself; for Jesus, self-pity could only weaken the resolution he absolutely needed to allow himself to be crucified.

To throw our own pity party is to wallow in our own weakness rather than finding our strength in Christ. Self-pity is simply an exercise in turning our back on God. Jesus didn't do it in his darkest moments; neither should we.

I appreciate the sentiment, but don't give us pity.
-- St. Louis Cardinals manager Mike Matheny

Adversity should lead us to God
and not to self-pity.

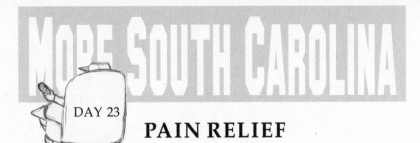

DAY 23

PAIN RELIEF

Read 2 Corinthians 1:3-7.

"Just as the sufferings of Christ flow over into our lives, so also through Christ our comfort overflows" (v. 5).

Apparently, the pain of a broken hand was no problem for Christian Walker.

In 2012, Walker led the national runners-up with a .327 average. He also led the squad in home runs and RBIs. He notched the same triple crown for the national champions of 2011; "there was no question who had carried the Carolina offense" that season.

The Gamecocks faced the real possibility, however, that their star would be on the bench for the championship series against Florida in the 2011 College World Series. In the bottom of the twelfth inning of the 3-2 win over Virginia that sent USC to the finals, Walker swung awkwardly through a curve ball. He flied out, and before he could even get off the field, his left hand was beginning to throb. "As soon as I stepped back in the dugout, the pain was crazy," Walker said. The trainer took a look and diagnosed a fractured hamate bone.

The Gamecocks had two days off, and Walker skipped workouts. Star pitcher Michael Roth asked Walker if he were going to play Monday against Florida. Walker nodded. "Yeah," Roth said. "You better."

The truth came out at batting practice Sunday afternoon when Walker took his first swing. "It was the worst pain I've ever felt," he said. The excruciating pain dropped Walker to his knees, and head coach Ray Tanner accepted the fact that he would be missing his best hitter for the championship series.

Doctors worked with Walker in attempts to alleviate the pain. Monday, he went back into the batting cage while thousands of Gamecock fans in the stands anxiously watched. He homered on his first swing. "Are you serious?" Tanner asked.

Walker not only played but he excelled, getting four hits in the two-game sweep of the Gators. "I'm not going to go 50 percent because my hand's hurting a little bit," he explained.

Since you live on Earth and not in Heaven, you are forced to play with pain as Christian Walker was. Whether it's a car wreck that left you shattered, the end of a relationship that left you battered, or a loved one's death that left you tattered -- pain finds you and challenges you to keep going.

While God's word teaches that you will reap what you sow, life also teaches that pain and hardship are not necessarily the result of personal failure. Pain in fact can be one of the tools God uses to mold your character and change your life.

What are you to do when you are hit full-speed by the awful pain that seems to choke the very will to live out of you? Where is your consolation, your comfort, and your help?

In almighty God, whose love will never fail. When life knocks you to your knees, you're closer to God than ever before.

Doing everything I can. It's in God's hands at this point.
-- Christian Walker tweet on chances of playing after his injury

When life hits you with pain, you can always turn to God for comfort, consolation, and hope.

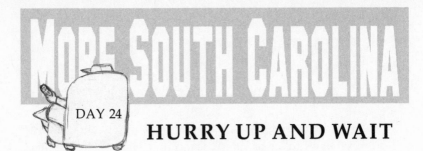

HURRY UP AND WAIT

Read Acts 1:1-14.

"Do not leave Jerusalem, but wait for the gift my Father promised, which you have heard me speak about" (v. 4).

Kelcy Quarles and his dad, Buddy, had long dreamed of Kelcy's playing football for South Carolina. When the time came, though, they had to wait a while longer.

"People see us and they say we look like brothers," Kelcy said of his father. "We're real tight." They have long been especially tight when it came to football.

Buddy Quarles played at USC as a 6-4, 330-lb. offensive tackle from 1984-87 under coach Joe Morrison. He unhesitatingly passed on his love of the Gamecocks to his son, often pulling out scrapbooks from his playing days. He also took Kelcy to games at Williams-Brice Stadium.

Thus, when the younger Quarles developed into an all-star defensive lineman, it came as no surprise that he committed to South Carolina at the end of his junior season. Unlike many who commit early, Kelcy never wavered as his dad and he waited for the time to come when he would don the garnet and black.

They had to wait longer than they expected, though, when Kelcy failed to qualify academically. Instead of heading to Columbia for the 2010 season, he wound up at Fork Union Military Academy in Virginia. Never, however, did he abandon the dream he shared with his father.

GAMECOCKS

After that longer wait, Kelcy Quarles took the field as a Gamecock in 2011. He was a force right away, moving into the starting lineup as a defensive tackle for the last six games. He was named to several Freshman All-America teams.

And was it worth the wait? Buddy thought so. "Oh, man, it's something else," he said. "That first game . . ., when he came running out on the field, I just burst into tears, me and my wife."

You rush to your doctor's appointment and wind up sitting in the appropriately named waiting room for an hour. You wait in the concessions line at a Gamecock game. You're put on hold when you call a tragically misnamed "customer service" center. All of that waiting is time in which we seem to do nothing but feel the precious minutes of our life ticking away.

Sometimes we even wait for God. We have needs, we call upon the Lord in our desperation, and then we are disappointed when we perhaps get no immediate answer.

But Jesus' last command to his disciples was to wait. Moreover, the entire of our Christian life is spent in an attitude of waiting for Jesus' return. While we wait for God, we hold steadfast to his promises, we continue our ministry, we remain in communion with him through prayer and devotion.

In other words, we don't just wait; we grow stronger in our faith. Waiting for God is never time lost.

He went the long road, but it was good for him.
-- Buddy Quarles on Kelcy's stint at Fork Union

Since God acts on his time and not ours,
we often must wait for him, using the time
to strengthen our faith.

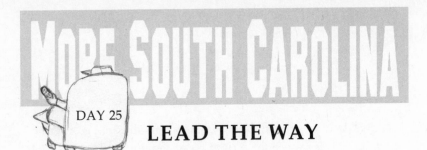
DAY 25

LEAD THE WAY

Read Matthew 16:18-23.

"You are Peter, and on this rock I will build my church, and the gates of Hades will not overcome it" (v. 18).

His teammates disliked him so much that a pitcher threw at him every time he faced him during fall camp. But Adrian Morales was the leader the Gamecocks needed to become champions.

Morales came to Columbia in the fall of 2009 from a Miami junior college, a brash kid raised in a tough neighborhood. Being Hispanic made him different. In addition, "he said words funny; he was loud and gruff; he had never heard of sweet tea."

Morales thought he suppressed his innate leadership qualities while he adjusted to South Carolina and it adjusted to him. He didn't really, though. "I hated Adrian. I hated him," said pitcher Michael Roth, the ace of the 2011 national champions and the 2012 national runners-up. "I just wasn't a fan."

Roth wasn't alone. Freshman Greg Harrison did his best to hit Morales every time he pitched to him during 2009's fall camp. But something happened when the real season started. "I loved him in the spring," Roth said.

Why the change? Because Morales wanted to win, and though the players didn't realize it, they needed a vocal leader. Morales was their guy; he was their in-your-face leader. "There were guys who would have to answer to him if there were some issues, and they didn't want to," said pitching coach Mark Calvi, who had discovered Morales and then recommended him to head coach Ray Tanner. "He took ownership of that team."

As the starting third baseman, Morales was the clutch hitter for the two-time national champions. Whit Merrifield said the team called him "Geico, because he always proved insurance."

That and the leadership the team needed to be more than just good -- to be champions.

Every aspect of life that involves people – every organization, every group, every project, every team -- must have a leader. If goals are to be reached, somebody must take charge.

Even the early Christian church was no different. Jesus knew this, so he designated the leader in Simon Peter, who was such an unlikely choice to assume such an awesome, world-changing responsibility that Jesus soon after rebuked him as "Satan."

In *Twelve Ordinary Men*, John MacArthur described Simon as "ambivalent, vacillating, impulsive, unsubmissive." Hardly a man to inspire confidence in his leadership skills. Yet, according to MacArthur, Peter became "the greatest preacher among the apostles" and the "dominant figure" in the birth of the church.

The implication for your own life is both obvious and unsettling. You may think you lack the attributes necessary to make a good leader for Christ. But consider Simon Peter, an ordinary man who allowed Christ to rule his life and became the foundation upon which the Christian church was built.

We couldn't have won without Adrian Morales's leadership.
-- USC pitching coach Mark Calvi

God's leaders are men and women
who allow Jesus to lead them.

DAY 26

SOMETHING NEW

Read Ephesians 4:17-24.

"You were taught . . . to put off your old self . . . and to put on the new self, created to be like God in true righteousness and holiness" (vv. 22, 24).

The 2010 Gamecocks, of course, blazed a trail for all subsequent USC baseball teams to follow. Nevertheless, the 2011 champions did something new at the College World Series, something even that 2010 bunch didn't pull off.

The Gamecocks opened the drive for a repeat national title in Omaha against Texas A&M on June 19. The Aggies immediately dropped a four-run bomb in the top of the first on Carolina and its ace, Michael Roth. The Gamecocks returned the favor in the bottom of the first, using a balk, an error, and three singles to put their own four-spot on the scoreboard.

As the Gamecocks trotted to their positions for the start of the second inning, third baseman Adrian Morales assembled his most intimidating scowl and approached Roth on the mound. He punched his pitcher in the chest and gruffly issued a command: "Hey, no more runs." Roth nodded.

And responded. When Roth came out of the game in the eighth inning, the Aggies hadn't scored again, having managed only two harmless singles after that rough first inning. Unfortunately, the Gamecocks hadn't scored any more either.

USC came to bat in the bottom of the ninth still involved in that 4-4 deadlock. Catcher Robert Beary, the MVP of the regional, got the inning off to a promising start by lashing a double. Jackie Bradley, Jr., followed with a single to left; third-base coach Chad Holbrook played it cautiously, holding Beary at third.

After Evan Marzilli walked, the bases were loaded for Scott "Walk-off" Wingo. He singled and Carolina had a win.

And that was the something new. The Gamecocks had lost all seven of their previous Omaha openers going back to 1977. Even head coach Ray Tanner was 0-4 in first games -- until then.

New things in our lives often have a life-changing effect. A new spouse. A new baby. A new job. Even something as mundane as a new television set or lawn mower jolts us with change.

While new experiences, new people, and new toys may make our lives new, they can't make new lives for us. Inside, where it counts – down in the deepest recesses of our soul – we're still the same, no matter how desperately we may wish to change.

An inner restlessness drives us to seek escape from a life that is a monotonous routine. Such a mundane existence just isn't good enough for someone who is a child of God; it can't even be called living. We want more out of life; something's got to change.

The only hope for a new life lies in becoming a brand new man or woman. And that is possible only through Jesus Christ, he who can make all things new again.

It's a very unusual feeling for me to be in Omaha and win the first game.
-- Ray Tanner after the opening-game win over A&M

A brand new you with the promise of a life worth living is waiting in Jesus Christ.

DAY 27

BLESS YOU

Read Romans 5:1-11.

"We also rejoice in our sufferings because we know that suffering produces perseverance; perseverance, character; and character, hope. And hope does not disappoint us" (vv. 3-5a).

T.J. Johnson is a blessed man, he knows it, and he doesn't mind going out of his way to tell others.

Unless injury determined otherwise, Johnson, the Gamecocks' starting center, set a school record in the 2012 season for most career starts. Entering his senior season, he had started all forty games in which he played, leaving him only seven games behind all-time leader Cliff Matthews, a defensive end.

What set Johnson apart from many of his peers was his appreciation for how blessed he was to have the skills to play major-college football. And his use of the fame he gained at Carolina to spread the word of God.

"I feel there is a reason why I was given the spotlight I have been given," Johnson said. "I can reach a whole lot of people because I'm a football player. God put me in this position."

Johnson grew up in Aynor being taken to church regularly by his parents. In high school he carried a copy of the Bible and read scripture during his free time. "I always have been the kind of guy that has not worried about what other people think," he said.

Originally reluctant to speak in public, Johnson was eased into it by his uncle, the team chaplains, and Jack Easterby, the director of the USC chapter of the Fellowship of Christian Athletes. "Public speaking is my biggest fear," declared the 6-foot-5, 305-lb. player.

Despite his fear, Johnson spoke about twenty times each off-season after his high school asked him to speak at a revival his freshman year and he realized the potential he could have for Christ. "All of a sudden, he's a rock star," said his dad.

T.J. Johnson is a very blessed "rock star" who uses his blessings as a means to spread the good news of Jesus Christ.

We just never know what God is up to. We can know, though, that he's always busy preparing blessings for us and that if we trust and obey him, he will pour out those blessings upon us.

Some of those blessings, however, come disguised as hardship and suffering. It is usually only from the perspective of hindsight -- after we have passed through them -- that we can understand how trials ultimately have blessed our life in the long run.

The key lies in trusting God, in realizing that God isn't out to destroy us but instead is interested only in doing good for us, even if that means allowing us to endure the consequences of a difficult lesson. God doesn't manage a candy store; more often, he relates to us as a stern but always loving father. If we truly love and trust God, no matter what our situation is now, he has blessings in store for us. This, above all, is our greatest hope.

Some have the heart of Christ, some might have the hand of Christ. T.J. [Johnson] has the mouth of Christ.
                                        -- Jack Easterby, FAC director at USC

Life's hardships are often transformed into blessings when we endure them trusting in God.

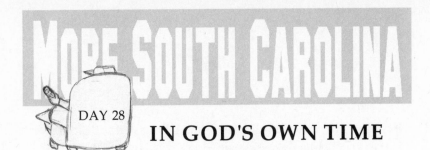

IN GOD'S OWN TIME

Read James 5:7-12.

"Be patient, then, brothers, until the Lord's coming" (v. 7).

Nolan Belcher learned all about patience in Columbia. After all, he went almost two years between starts for the Gamecock baseball team.

The left-hander from Augusta was 4-5 and made thirteen starts for the 2009 Gamecocks and was named to the All-SEC Freshman Team. He was sterling in 2010 for the national champions with a 3-1 record and a 2.43 ERA in eleven games. On May 26, he started against Ole Miss, the last of his six starts that season.

Belcher had high expectations for his junior season, but they never materialized. In January 2011, he blew out his left elbow and underwent surgery. He missed the entire season.

He returned to make ten relief appearances for the 2012 team until April 10 when head coach Ray Tanner tabbed him the starter against The Citadel. When he threw his first pitch, it had been six weeks and change short of two years since his last start.

Tanner said the junior had earned the start. "He hasn't had as many opportunities [to pitch] as we wanted to give him," the head coach said. Pitching coach Jerry Myers "made the suggestion that we get him [to] the mound for this start and get him 75 pitches."

Belcher admitted that the wait with its months of rehabilitation had been long and had often tried his patience. With each appearance in 2012, though, he had regained a measure of confidence; he was ready for the start.

The results proved it. Belcher worked 5 2/3 scoreless innings in the 8-0 USC win. Only one Citadel runner reached second base. He left the game after throwing 86 pitches and earned the win.

Belcher's patience paid off with a good year for USC. He got one more start in 2012 and appeared in nineteen games overall. He had a 4-2 record with a 2.12 ERA for the national runners-up.

Have you ever left a restaurant because the server didn't take your order quickly enough? Complained at your doctor's office about how long you had to wait? Wondered how much longer a sermon was going to last?

It isn't just the machinations of the world with which we're impatient; we want God to move at our pace, not his. For instance, how often have you prayed and expected – indeed, demanded – an immediate answer from God? And aren't Christians the world over impatient for the glorious day when Jesus will return and set everything right? We're in a hurry but God obviously isn't.

As rare as it seems to be, patience is nevertheless included among the likes of gentleness, humility, kindness, and compassion as attributes of a Christian.

God expects us to be patient. He knows what he's doing, he is in control, and his will shall be done. On his schedule, not ours.

I was born and raised on a farm, and when you watch those crops grow, you learn to be patient.
-- Former Auburn football coach and athletic director Pat Dye

God moves in his own time, so often we must wait for him to act, remaining faithful and patient.

DAY 29

UNCERTAIN TIMES

Read Psalm 18:1-6, 20-29.

"The Lord is my rock . . . in whom I take refuge. He is my shield, and the horn of my salvation, my stronghold" (v. 2).

Standing on the edge of the first men's national title in the school's history is a logical place for a coach to feel uncertain, especially when grabbing that championship may well ride on his decision. But Chad Holbrook was not uncertain at all.

On June 29, 2010, the South Carolina Gamecocks needed only to beat UCLA to win the NCAA national championship in baseball. The Bruins scored first, and Carolina missed some scoring chances early. In the bottom of the eighth, pinch runner Robert Beary scored when shortstop Bobby Haney's shot skipped off the first-baseman's glove for an error. The game was tied.

The teams battled into the bottom of the eleventh, still tied at one. Junior Scott Wingo, who set the school record for walks that season, led off the inning with a free pass. The first pitch to Evan Marzilli skipped off the catcher's mitt to the backstop. Wingo moved up. Marzilli then laid down a bunt to move Wingo to third.

Holbrook, the associate head coach, was there waiting for him, and the coach was running through his mind all the possibilities. How should he play it if junior right fielder Whit Merrifield hit a shallow fly ball or a high chopper in the infield? Then Holbrook realized that the Bruins would never let Jackie Bradley, Jr., the

GAMECOCKS

on-deck batter and the College World Series MVP, have a chance to win the game. They would walk him no matter what.

That realization removed all uncertainty Holbrook had about what to do. "We had to be aggressive at third," he decided. "We were going to try to score. This was our chance." Wingo likewise was certain, saying, "We're gonna do this, Coach!"

The Gamecocks certainly did. Merrifield singled, and Wingo trotted home with the national title.

Even when we believe the Gamecocks will field a good team, we have some uncertainty because baseball just isn't a sure thing. If it were, it wouldn't be any fun.

But life itself is much like a game between two top-ten teams. We never know what's in store for us or what's going to happen next. We can be riding high one day with a job promotion, good health, a nice family, and sunny weather. Only a short time later, we can be unemployed, sick, divorced, and/or broke.

When we place our trust in life itself and its rewards, we are certain to face uncertain times.

We must search out a haven, a place where we know we can find shelter when life's storms buffet us and knock us down. Right there on our knees, we can find that rock. Right there on our knees, we can find that certainty – every time.

Our life and times are uncertain. The Lord God Almighty is sure – and is only a prayer away.

All of those thoughts, and so many more, were going through my head.
-- Chad Holbrook with Scott Wingo on third in the 11th inning

The world is an uncertain place;
only God offers certainty no matter what happens.

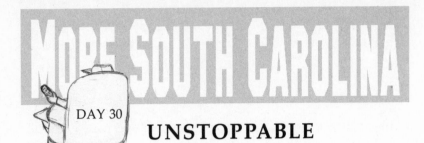
DAY 30

UNSTOPPABLE

Read Acts 5:29-42.

"If it is from God, you will not be able to stop these men; you will only find yourselves fighting against God" (v. 39).

Defensive end Melvin Ingram was unstoppable in the win over Georgia in 2011. And not just on the line; he was unstoppable as a running back, too.

On Sept. 10, the Gamecocks had their last early-season show-down with the Bulldogs. (Beginning in 2012 the game was moved to later in the season.) It was one of the best in the long, competitive series, an offensive thriller with Ingram scoring what turned out to be the game-winning touchdown.

USC led 38-35 late in the game when Ingram's fellow defensive end, Jadeveon Clowney, nailed the Dog quarterback and stripped him of the ball. Ingram scooped the loose pigskin up at the UGA 5 and strolled into the end zone for a 45-35 lead with just three minutes left. After Georgia scored, Ingram recovered the onside kick to drive the last nail in the Bulldog coffin. USC won 45-42.

All that was certainly outstanding enough, but what Ingram pulled off in the second quarter can truly best be described as "unstoppable." UGA led 13-7 when the Gamecocks faked a punt with a direct snap to Ingram. He deftly avoided a tackle at the line of scrimmage, angled toward the sideline, and took off.

Just watching 267 pounds of Gamecock football player literally sprint down the sideline was amazing enough, but when a Bulldog cornerback tried to tackle him at the 35, Ingram jumped over him! He then jaunted on into the end zone to complete a 68-yard touchdown. As Gamecock defensive coordinator Ellis Johnson observed, "That wasn't a punter or a kickoff guy trying to tackle [Ingram]. That's an NFL corner."

"I try to do it all," is what Ingram had to say about the Georgia game. "He's a ballplayer," an admiring head coach Steve Spurrier said about his unstoppable senior.

Wouldn't we like our life to unfold pretty much as the record-setting 2011 USC football season did? One success after another in our career, our family, our investments – whatever we tackle. Unstoppable. The reality is, though, that life isn't like that at all. At some point, we all run into setbacks that stop us dead in our tracks; the Gamecocks did in 2011. Everyone does – except God.

For almost two thousand years, the enemies of God have tried to stop Jesus and his people. They killed Jesus; they have persecuted and martyred his followers. Today, heretics and infidels – many of them in America -- are more active in their war on Christianity than at any other time in history.

And yet, the Kingdom of God advances, unstoppable despite all opposition. Pursuing God's purposes in our lives puts us on a team bound for glory. Fighting against God gets his enemies nowhere. Except Hell.

Melvin's a great athlete. He can do about anything.
* -- USC defensive coordinator Ellis Johnson after the UGA game*

**God's kingdom and purposes are unstoppable
no matter what his enemies try.**

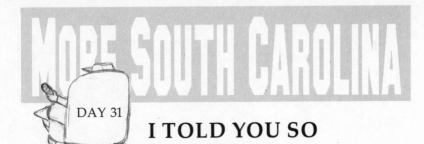

DAY 31

I TOLD YOU SO

Read Matthew 24:15-31.

"See, I have told you ahead of time" (v. 25).

When Brian Scott told his head coach, Lou Holtz, that he would catch the ball, he didn't know he would make one of the most memorable plays in South Carolina football history.

Scott was the Gamecocks' leading receiver and a co-captain as a senior in 2001. Carolina won nine games that season, including a win over Ohio State in the Outback Bowl.

In a defensive struggle against Georgia in Athens on Sept. 8, the Bulldogs led 9-7 as the clock ticked away the fourth quarter. With 1:28 left in the game, the Gamecocks faced a third and ten at the Georgia 16. That's when Scott spoke up.

On the sideline, he told Holtz that he wanted the ball. "I told him I could beat my man," Scott said. "It may have been the only time I ever said that to a coach but I wanted the ball."

Holtz agreed with Scott's memory of the play. "There's no doubt about it," the former head coach said. "When we were discussing what to do, he said he wanted the ball."

So the coaches called a play that sent Scott out as the only receiver, and he did exactly what he said he would do. He beat his defender to the corner and then reached around the Bulldog to haul in a desperate pass from pressured quarterback Phil Petty.

Scott's only worry on the play was whether or not he was in the end zone. He was, by about a yard. He had made what became known in Gamecock lore as "The Catch." When he rose from the turf and the official's hands went up, the packed stadium went eerily quiet. The score stood up as USC won 14-9.

To Scott's amazement, fans still talked about the play more than ten years after he made it. "When I go to the games," he said in an interview in 2011, "people always come up to me and talk about it. It's one of the biggest catches in Gamecock history."

And it happened because he told his coaches he would do it.

Unless it's a Gamecock like Brian Scott who produces on the field as he said he would, don't you just hate it in when somebody says, "I told you so"? That means the other person was right and you were wrong; that other person has spoken the truth. You could have listened to that know-it-all in the first place, but then you would have lost the chance yourself to crow, "I told you so."

In our pluralistic age and society, many view truth as relative, meaning absolute truth does not exist. All belief systems have equal value and merit. But this is a ghastly, dangerous fallacy because it ignores the truth that God proclaimed in the presence and words of Jesus.

In speaking the truth, Jesus told everybody exactly what he was going to do: come back and take his faithful followers with him. Those who don't listen or who don't believe will be left behind with those four awful words, "I told you so," ringing in their ears and wringing their souls.

He was our most experienced guy and he wanted the ball.
-- Lou Holtz, discussing 'The Catch'

Jesus matter-of-factly told us what he has planned:
He will return to gather all the faithful to himself.

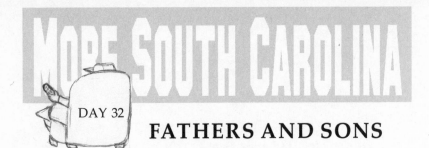

DAY 32

FATHERS AND SONS

Read Luke 3:1-22.

"And a voice came from heaven: 'You are my Son, whom I love; with you I am well pleased'" (v. 22).

David Roth wasn't about to miss seeing his son, Michael, pitch in the 2011 College World Series -- even if getting to Omaha meant he had to quit his job.

Michael Roth was the ace of the Gamecock pitching staff in 2011 and 2012. (See Devotion No. 66.) He also had a pair of starts in the 2010 College World Series, his first two of the season. He beat Clemson 5-1 with a complete game and then allowed only one run in six innings with a no-decision in the championship-clinching win over UCLA.

Roth's dad missed both of those games. A car salesman, the demands of work kept him at home in Greer. He wasn't about to let that happen again. So, after the Gamecocks waxed Connecticut 8-2 to win the Super Regional and punch their ticket to Omaha in 2011, Roth's mom told him his dad would be in the stands for USC's opening game, which Roth would start.

Roth figured his dad would simply use some vacation days to make the trip. At a family dinner in Omaha the night before his start, Roth learned otherwise. His dad had actually quit his job so he could come to Omaha. As Roth related it, the bosses at work told his dad he didn't have any vacation days. "[Dad] said, 'I've got to go out there to Omaha,' so he just quit." That Saturday

GAMECOCKS

night, Roth tweeted, "How's this for dedication? My dad had to quit his job to make it out to Omaha."

So a dedicated but unemployed David Roth was there to watch his son pitch into the seventh inning against Texas A&M without giving up an earned run. The Gamecocks won 5-4 and were on their way to the national title.

Contemporary American society largely belittles and marginalizes fathers and their influence upon their sons. Men are perceived as necessary to effect pregnancy; after that, they can leave and everybody's better off.

But we need look in only two places to appreciate the enormity of that misconception: our jails – packed with males who lacked the influence of fathers in their lives as they grew up -- and the Bible. God – being God – could have chosen any relationship he desired between Jesus and himself, including society's approach of irrelevancy. Instead, the most important relationship in all of history was that of father-son

God obviously believes a close, loving relationship between fathers and sons, like that of David and Michael Roth, is crucial. For men and women to espouse otherwise or for men to walk blithely and carelessly out of their children's lives constitutes disobedience to the divine will.

Simply put, God loves fathers. After all, he is one.

My dad's been a huge inspiration for baseball for me.
-- Michael Roth

Fatherhood is a tough job, but a model for the father-child relationship is found in that of Jesus the Son with God the Father.

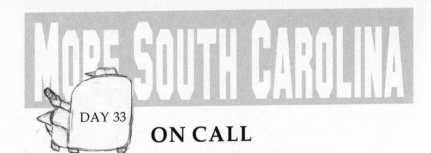

DAY 33

ON CALL

Read 1 Samuel 3:1-18.

"The Lord came and stood there, calling as at the other times, 'Samuel! Samuel!' Then Samuel said, 'Speak, for your servant is listening'" (v. 10).

Something sort of peculiar happened in the last part of defensive end Devin Taylor's sophomore season: He quit getting quarterback sacks -- and the coaches were quite happy about it.

After a redshirt season, Taylor became a part-time starter in 2009 and then nailed down a starting spot on his own in 2010. He led all USC defensive linemen with 46 tackles and was first-team All-SEC. After thirteen more starts as a junior, he entered 2012 in the top ten in Gamecock history in sacks and tackles for loss.

Taylor got off to a great start rushing the quarterback in 2010 and would eventually lead the team in quarterback hurries. In the first eight games, he registered 6 1/2 sacks and appeared to be on his way to leading the conference. Then something happened. Through the next five games, he had only one sack.

So what happened? Well, the coaches did.

They decided to take better advantage of Taylor's skills, asking him to drop back more often in pass coverage, which, of course, meant fewer chances to drop a quarterback. When the Gamecocks shifted from a traditional four-man front to a three-man rush in a passing situation, Taylor, who is 6-foot-8, was the lineman chosen to drop back into coverage.

GAMECOCKS

Defensive line coach Brad Lawing's explanation for the move was simple. "We try to put our players in the best possible position, and he [drops into coverage] better than anybody we've got [on the line]," Lawing said.

So how did Taylor feel about a move that limited his chances to pull off one of the game's more exciting and noteworthy plays? He never complained and gave the move his best, which turned out to be very good. Answering the call for the team, Taylor led the East Division champions in pass breakups with eight.

A team player is someone such as Devin Taylor who does whatever the coach calls upon him to do for the good of the team. Something quite similar occurs when God places a specific call upon a Christian's life.

This is much scarier, though, than changing assignments on a football field. Many folks understand that answering God's call means going into the ministry, packing the family up, and moving halfway around the world to some place where folks have never heard of air conditioning, fried chicken, paved roads, or the Gamecocks. Zambia. The Philippines. Cleveland even.

Not for you, no thank you. And who can blame you?

But the truth is that God usually calls folks to serve him where they are. In fact, God put you where you are right now, and he has a purpose in placing you there. Wherever you are, you are called to serve him.

He's a team player, completely.
-- Defensive line coach Brad Lawing on Devin Taylor

God calls you to serve him right now right where he has put you, wherever that is.

DAY 34

FAIL-SAFE

Read Luke 22:54-62.

"Peter remembered the word the Lord had spoken to him: 'Before the rooster crows today, you will disown me three times.' And he went outside and wept bitterly" (vv. 61b-62).

Gamecock pitching coach Mark Calvi knew that he was doing something he never really wanted to do with his pitchers: He was setting Matt Price up for failure.

Forced to redshirt in 2009 because of a wrist injury, Price was a mystery entering the 2010 season. He was so bad in fall camp that Calvi told him he would be the eleventh man on the ten-man staff. "From the second he heard that, it was all over," Calvi said.

Price responded to the criticism by going to the weight room in earnest. The increased strength translated to a fast ball that reached 95 miles an hour. Early in the season, Calvi experimented by calling on Price in a 4-4 game in the eighth inning. He got out of a jam and got the win. By April, Price was the team's closer.

Entering the super regional, Price had eight saves, but he had never encountered anything like what Calvi threw at him in the first game against Coastal Carolina. The Gamecocks led 4-3 in the eighth inning, but the Chanticleers had the bases loaded with no outs. The first batter had more home runs and RBIs than anyone on the USC roster. It was not a good situation for a pitcher.

Calvi understood he was not doing Price any favors. "This is the worst possible situation you could ever be in," the veteran coach thought. He was keenly aware that he was violating one of his basic principles: never put a pitcher in a position to fail.

But Price didn't see it that way. He wanted the ball to show how good he was. And he did. Head coach Ray Tanner admitted after the game that Price would have done a great job if he had just held Coastal to one run. A tied game would have been a relief.

Instead, Price struck out the first two batters and then got the last out on a grounder back to him. Set up to fail, Price succeeded wildly. He then pitched a scoreless ninth to nail down the save.

Failure is usually defined by expectations. A baseball player who hits .300 is a star, but he fails seventy percent of the time. We grumble about a postal system that manages to deliver billions of items without a hitch.

And we are often our own harshest critics, beating ourselves up for our failings because we expected better. Never mind that our expectations were unrealistic to begin with.

The bad news about life is that failure – unlike success -- is inevitable. Only one man walked this earth perfectly and we're not him. The good news about life, however, is that failure isn't permanent. In life, we always have time to reverse our failures as did Peter, he who failed our Lord so abjectly.

The same cannot be said of death. In death we eternally suffer the consequences of our failure to follow that one perfect man.

That's the worst thing you can do to a kid.
-- Mark Calvi on setting up Matt Price to fail vs. Coastal Carolina

Only one failure in life dooms us to eternal failure in death: failing to follow Jesus Christ.

JUGGERNAUT

Read Revelation 20.

*"Fire came down from heaven and devoured them. And
the devil, who deceived them, was thrown into the lake of
burning sulfur, where the beast and the false prophet had
been thrown" (vv. 9b-10a).*

The Vanderbilt Commodores ran into a juggernaut they weren't
expecting. Neither was anybody else.

On Sept. 24, 2011, the undefeated and 12th-ranked Gamecocks
took on a 3-0 Vanderbilt squad that had averaged 33 points and
318 yards per game. On the other side of the ball, the Gamecock
defense had struggled "mightily" against East Carolina, Georgia,
and Navy. The Carolina defense was certainly no juggernaut.

Well, not until the Vanderbilt game.

In one of the most impressive defensive showings in decades,
the Gamecock defense completely shut down the Commodore
offense. Vanderbilt gained a grand total of 77 yards for the entire
game, which, according to one researcher, was the second-fewest
yards allowed by the Gamecocks since at least 1966. The USC
defense even outscored the Vandy offense in the 21-3 win.

Neither offense, in fact, was up to much all afternoon. Head
Gamecock Steve Spurrier apologized to the fans after the game
for what he called "a putrid offensive performance."

The USC offense even contributed to Vanderbilt's early 3-0 lead.
The field goal was courtesy of a drive that covered only six yards

GAMECOCKS

after an interception. With 11:59 left in the half, though, defensive lineman Melvin Ingram put his mitts around a Vandy fumble in the end zone for a touchdown. With a juggernaut defense on the field, the Gamecocks had enough points to win the game.

The USC defense that came into the game giving up 33 points and 372 yards per encounter grudgingly surrendered only five first downs the whole game and had six sacks. Helpless against the juggernaut, Vandy averaged a miniscule 1.6 yards per play and managed a grand total of -4 yards rushing in the first half.

Maybe your experience with a juggernaut involved a game against a team packed with major college prospects, a league tennis match against a former college player, or your presentation for the project you knew didn't stand a chance. Whatever it was, you've been slam-dunked before.

Being part of a juggernaut is certainly more fun than being in the way of one. Just ask Vanderbilt against USC in 2011. Or consider the forces of evil aligned against God. At least the Commodores had some hope, however slim, that they might win. No such hope exists for those who oppose God.

That's because their fate is already spelled out in detail. It's in the book; we all know how the story ends. God's enemies may talk big and bluster now, but they will be soundly trounced and routed in the most decisive defeat of all time.

You sure want to be on the winning side in that one.

That was a super defensive game.
                                  -- Steve Spurrier after the 2011 Vandy game

**The most lopsided victory in all of history
will be God's ultimate triumph over evil.**

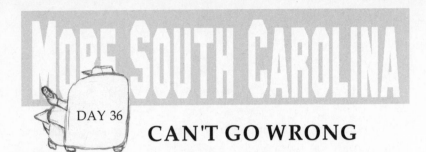

DAY 36

CAN'T GO WRONG

Read Galatians 6:7-10.

"Let us not grow weary in doing what is right, for we will reap at harvest time, if we do not give up" (v. 9 NRSV).

Though it involved risk for his team, Ray Tanner did the right thing and helped out a friend.

In May 2011, as his Gamecocks were winning their way toward their second straight national championship, Tanner got a phone call from Art Inabinet. The head baseball coach at Francis Marion had an unusual request: Would Tanner bring his Gamecocks to Florence in 2012 to play a single game against the Patriots?

Inabinet's solicitation was unique in that Francis Marion is a Division II program. Major college powerhouses -- especially the reigning national champions -- would rarely, if ever, even consider playing a Division II team on its home turf. In his sixteen seasons at USC, Tanner had never played a Division II team anywhere.

As both Tanner and Inabinet appreciated, playing the Patriots would have no upside at all for the Gamecocks. Coaches must always keep an eye on the Ratings Percentage Index (RPI), used by the NCAA to rank teams and thus decide slots and seedings for postseason play. In USC's case, a win over the Patriots wouldn't help the RPI, and a loss would certainly hurt it.

But Inabinet had a good reason for his unlikely request. The Patriots were opening a new stadium in 2012, and he wanted to make the game special. The Gamecocks would do just that, virtually ensuring a sellout. After a pause, Tanner replied, "Sure, I think that's something we can work out." The coach figured the risk was worth it to help promote baseball in the state. Plus, he said, "I like the atmosphere and the energy of a new ballpark."

Sure enough, the game was sold out well in advance. And the Patriots, who were ranked 20th in Division II, delighted the home crowd by pulling off the 5-4 upset of the 9th-ranked Gamecocks.

Tanner's doing the right thing didn't hurt one bit as the 2012 Gamecocks made school history by advancing to the finals of the world series for the third straight year.

Doing the right thing is easy when it's little stuff. Giving the quarter back when the cashier gives you too much change, helping a lost child at the mall, or putting a few bucks in the honor box at your favorite fishing hole.

But what about when it costs you? Every day you have chances to do the right thing; in every instance, you have a choice: right or wrong. The factors that weigh into your decisions – including the personal cost to you – reveal much about your character.

Does your doing the right thing ever depend upon your calculation of the odds of getting caught? In the world's eyes, you can't go wrong doing wrong when you won't get caught. That passes for the world's slippery, situational ethics, but it certainly doesn't pass muster with God.

In God's eyes, you can't go wrong doing right. Ever.

I did it for the right reasons.
                    -- Ray Tanner on playing Francis Marion at their place

**As far as God is concerned,
you can never go wrong doing right.**

DAY 37

THE BIG TIME

Read Revelation 21:22-27; 22:1-6.

"They will see his face, and his name will be on their foreheads. . . . And they will reign for ever and ever" (vv. 22:4, 5c).

Tyler Hull was a college kicker, but it wasn't enough. He wanted the big time, so he headed to Columbia.

A native of Andy Griffith's Mt. Airy, which competes in North Carolina's smallest classification, Hull didn't receive much attention from college coaches even though he was a pretty good kicker in high school. He was a two-time all-state selection, and as a senior in 2009, he led the state's kickers with 118 points.

Nevertheless, he wound up in 2010 in Greensboro at Guilford College, a Division III school, because it was, as Hull put it, "my only option at the time." He had three field goals that season and punted in the season's final game, pounding one kick for 42 yards. The experience wasn't particularly enjoyable for Hull, however, as Guilford went 0-10.

During the season, though, Hull looked around and figured he was the best kicker in the conference. He decided he should give kicking at the highest levels a chance. A transfer that involved moving up in college football's hierarchy meant Hull had to sit out a year, but he didn't waste the time. He attended a number of kicking camps to improve his hang time and to get noticed by some of the more prominent schools. He also sent out a batch of e-mails. In the spring of 2012, South Carolina responded, offering him the chance to be a preferred walk-on. Hull took it.

He arrived in Columbia three days after preseason practices began to find himself number three on the depth chart. By the first scrimmage, though, head coach Steve Spurrier had declared, "It appears [Hull] may be our punter this year."

On Aug. 20, 2012, Hull hit the big time as USC's punter in the season-opening win over Vanderbilt.

Like Tyler Hull, we often look around at our current situation and dream of hitting the big time. We might look longingly at that vice-president's office or daydream about the day when we're the boss, maybe even of our own business. We may scheme about ways to make a lot of money, or at least more than we're making now. We may even consciously seek out fame and power.

Making it big is just part of the American dream. It's the heart of that which drives immigrants to leave everything they know and come to this country.

The truth is, though, is that all of this "big-time" stuff we so earnestly cherish is small potatoes. If we want to speak of what is the real big-time, we better think about God and his dwelling place in Heaven. There we not only see God and Jesus face to face, but we reign. God puts us in charge.

It just doesn't get any bigger than that – and it's ours for the taking. Or at least for the believing.

I might as well try to achieve something higher and see if it works out.
-- Tyler Hull on his decision to try big-time football

Living with God, seeing Jesus, and reigning in Heaven – now that's big time.

THE 'I' IN PRIDE

Read 1 John 2:15-17.

"Everything in the world -- the desire of the flesh, the desire of the eyes, the pride in riches -- comes not from the Father but from the world" (v. 16 NRSV).

You would think a whipping of Mississippi State during the regular season would not exactly be the kind of moment that would convince the USC coaches they had a team they could be proud of -- but it was.

When the Gamecocks rolled into Starkville on April 21, 2011, they were 29-7 and ranked second in the country. Chances for a repeat of the national title looked pretty good. The beat went right on in the opening game of the series, an 8-2 romp. Then on Saturday, things went painfully awry for the Gamecocks.

First, outfielder Evan Marzilli wound up in the intensive care unit with an intermittent rapid heartbeat. It took doctors a while to determine his condition was not life-threatening, but he would need surgery back home. Then another starting outfielder, Adam Matthews, suffered a recurrence of a pesky hamstring problem.

But it got worse. In the sixth inning of Saturday's game, Jackie Bradley, Jr., the team's all-star center fielder, landed awkwardly on his left wrist attempting a diving catch. He left the game and would also need surgery. His college career appeared over.

USC not only lost that game but its entire starting outfield. Before Sunday's series finale, head coach Ray Tanner told his team this would not be a time when they could sit around and moan and complain. "Let's go have some fun and do the best we can with what we've got and win anyway," he urged.

Incredibly, they did just that. Using a lineup loaded with part-time players, the Gamecocks blasted the Bulldogs 13-4, a win that "under those conditions defied logic." "If I've ever had a special feeling with this team," a proud assistant coach Chad Holbrook said, "it was the Sunday bus ride from Mississippi State."

What are you most proud of? The size of your bank account? The trophies from your tennis league? The title under your name at the office? Your family?

Pride is one of life's great paradoxes. You certainly want a heart surgeon who takes pride in her work or a USC coach who is proud of his team's accomplishments. But pride in the things and the people of this world is inevitably disappointing because it leads to dependence upon things that will pass away and idolization of people who will fail you. Self-pride is even more dangerous because it inevitably leads to self-glorification.

Pride in the world's baubles and its people lures you to the earthly and the temporary, and away from God and the eternal. Pride in yourself yields the same results in that you exalt yourself and not God. God alone is glorious enough to be worshipped. Jesus Christ alone is Lord.

You've answered the call, and I'm proud of you.
-- Ray Tanner to his team after the 13-4 win over Miss. State

Pride can be dangerous because it tempts you
to lower your sight from God and the eternal
to the world and the temporary.

DAY 39

HANGING IN THERE

Read Mark 14:32-42.

"'Father,' he said, 'everything is possible for you. Take this cup from me. Yet not what I will, but what you will'" (v. 36).

He was redshirted when he didn't want to be, spent a season on the bench, and had a transfer beat him out of his starting job. Kyle Enders persisted, though, and wound up with a season that surpassed all his dreams.

As a senior catcher in 2010, Enders had two great honors bestowed upon him. First, along with Jay Brown, his teammates voted him a team captain. Second, head coach Ray Tanner gave Enders the freedom to call the pitches. Asked how many catchers other than Enders he had allowed to call their own games, the veteran coach had a succinct reply: "Very few." He allowed Enders to do so, however, because of his confidence in the fifth-year player. "It comes down to years of experience and intelligence," Tanner explained.

That intelligence and experience were by-products of Enders' persistence. He refused to quit even when it looked on more than one occasion as though Columbia would never be the place where he would succeed as a baseball player.

Enders arrived on campus in the fall of 2005 and was promptly redshirted, a decision that he didn't like at all. He stayed around, though, and in 2007 saw action in 22 games. He appeared to be on his way in 2008 when he was the starting catcher and hit .260.

All his dreams fell apart, however, when transfer Justin Dalles showed up and booted Enders to the bench. Again Enders persevered, resolving to make the most of the situation. "He handled [Dalles' arrival] with tremendous class and dignity," Tanner said.

All that perseverance paid off in 2010 when Enders hit .281 as a vital cog of the national title team. When it was all over, he said, "It's been more than I expected. It's been a dream come true."

Life is tough; it inevitably beats us up and kicks us around some. But life has four quarters, and so here we are, still standing, still in the game. Like Kyle Enders and the Gamecocks, we know that we can never win if we don't finish. We emerge as winners and champions only if we never give up, if we just see it through.

Interestingly, Jesus has been in the same situation. On that awful night in the garden, Jesus understood the nature of the suffering he was about to undergo, and he begged God to take it from him. In the end, though, he yielded to God's will and surrendered his own.

Even in the matter of persistence, Jesus is our example. As he did, we push doggedly and determinedly ahead – following God's will for our lives -- no matter how hard it gets. And we can do it because God is with us.

I didn't want to redshirt, but looking back now, it's the best thing to happen to me. I couldn't have planned it any better.
— Kyle Enders on his Gamecock career

It's tough to keep going no matter what, but you have the power of almighty God to pull you through.

DAY 40

GOD'S CONQUERORS

Read John 16:19-33.

"In this world you will have trouble. But take heart! I have overcome the world" (v. 33b).

South Carolina's dreams of a great football season in 2011 died in Starkville only seven games into the schedule. Nobody however, bothered to inform the Gamecocks, who overcame the odds to win eleven games.

On Oct. 15, Mississippi State led 12-7 in the fourth quarter, and the Gamecock offense wasn't doing much. What was distressing was the reason why the offense was struggling. Sophomore running back Marcus Lattimore, "the heart of the [USC] offense," was on the sideline, and he wasn't receiving any last-minute, game-changing instructions from his coaches. Rather, he was receiving hugs and condolences from his mother as he sat with a knee wrapped in ice after being injured earlier in the game.

With Lattimore out, "an offense that had looked so brilliant one week ago against Kentucky suddenly had returned to the 'putrid' status so deemed by Steve Spurrier in a win against Vanderbilt." Without Lattimore and with star wide receiver Alshon Jeffery blanketed, the Gamecocks really didn't have much of a chance.

Somehow, though, they found a way to win, putting together a 12-play, 79-yard, game-winning drive to snatch a 14-12 win away from State. Connor Shaw, who completed 20 of his 28 passes but for only 155 yards, hit Jeffery with a 4-yard score that was the difference. Safety D.J. Swearinger finished off the Bulldogs with an interception on their last possession.

Shortly after Shaw spoke at the postgame news conference, Lattimore hobbled through the room on crutches, his season over. As the win over State showed, though, the team's season didn't limp out the door with him. The Gamecocks would overcome.

We each have a choice to make about how we live. We can merely survive or we can overcome as the 2011 Gamecocks did.

We frequently hear inspiring stories of people who triumph by overcoming especially daunting obstacles. Those barriers may be physical or mental disabilities or great personal tragedies or injustice. When we hear of them, we may well respond with a little prayer of thanksgiving that life has been kinder to us.

But all people of faith, no matter how drastic the obstacles they face, must ultimately overcome the same opponent: the Satan-infested world. Some do have it tougher than others, but we all must fight daily to remain confident and optimistic.

To merely survive from day to day is to give up by surrendering our trust in God's involvement in our daily life. To overcome, however, is to stand up to the world and fight its temptations that would erode the armor of our faith in Jesus Christ.

Today is a day for you to overcome by remaining faithful. The very hosts of Heaven wait to hail the conquering hero.

You think, if enough bad things are happening, it would be difficult to win the game, but our guys hung in there.
-- Steve Spurrier on the win over Mississippi State

Life's difficulties provide us a chance to experience the true joy of victory in Jesus.

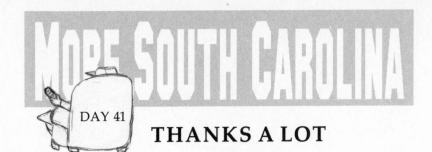

DAY 41

THANKS A LOT

Read 1 Thessalonians 5:12-28.

"[G]ive thanks in all circumstances, for this is God's will for you in Christ Jesus" (v. 18).

In the wake of USC's 2010 NCAA baseball title, head coach Ray Tanner singled out three people to thank. Two might have been expected; the third would have been unknown to anyone not closely connected with the team and its season.

The first person Tanner thanked was the late Sarge Frye, a fixture in USC's athletic department for forty-five years. The second was the late Tom Price, the school's sports information director for thirty years. And then there was Bayler Teal.

In September 2008, Bayler was diagnosed with a common form of childhood cancer. Learning of him through a former player, the baseball team decided to adopt the Teal family for Christmas that year. Over time, the players visited him in the hospital and talked to him on the phone. He called the Gamecocks his friends.

In April 2010, the players learned that the boy's health was deteriorating. They dedicated a three-game series at Georgia to him. "They're playing -- for me?" Bayler told his dad. USC won all three games. In June, doctors said nothing more could be done for Bayler; the Gamecocks vowed to keep on playing for him.

On June 24, they faced an elimination game against Oklahoma in the College World Series. They trailed 2-1 in the bottom of the twelfth inning and were down to their last strike when Jackie

Bradley, Jr., singled to tie the game. Two batters later, Brady Thomas' single drove Bradley home with the winning run.

The players learned minutes later that Bayler had died at 9:32, just as the Gamecocks scored their first run in the game. He was 7 years old. The timing of their talisman's death was no coincidence, the players said. "When he passed, we felt like we had something behind us then," said Bayler's favorite player, Whit Merrifield. "We thought that we weren't going to lose."

They didn't. And so Tanner thanked Bayler.

Thank you, Lord, for my cancer. Thank you, Lord, for my unemployment. Thank you, Lord, that my children are in trouble with the law. Is this what the Bible means when it tells us to always be thankful?

Of course not. As a man of reasonably good sense, Paul didn't tell us to give thanks for everything that happens to us, but to give thanks to God even when bad things occur. The joy we know in our soul through Jesus, the prayers we offer to God, and the gratitude we feel for the blessings that are in our lives even in the midst of distress – these don't fluctuate with our circumstances.

Failure to thank God implies that we believe we alone are responsible for the good things in our lives. Such arrogance relegates God to the fringes of our lives. An attitude of gratitude, however, keeps God right where he belongs in our lives: at its heart and soul.

I felt Bayler's hand on my bat.
-- Scott Wingo on his title-winning hit against UCLA

No matter what, we can always be thankful
for God's presence.

DAY 42

UNBELIEVABLE!

Read Hebrews 3:7-19.

"See to it, brothers, that none of you has a sinful, unbelieving heart that turns away from the living God" (v. 12).

In an unbelievable finish, the Gamecocks won a game in the 2011 College World Series when a player -- hindered by a hamstring injury -- scored from second on a bunt.

USC's game against top-ranked Virginia on June 24 in Omaha was described as "one of the strangest and best games in the history of the College World Series." With the winner advancing to the championship series against Florida and the loser going home, UVa led 1-0 early, but the Gamecocks rallied in the bottom of the fourth. Senior catcher Brady Thomas dropped a one-out double to left that scored Christian Walker and Jackie Bradley, Jr., for a 2-1 lead.

The Gamecocks nursed that slim lead until the eighth when the Cavaliers scratched out a run. UVa went on to load the bases against USC closer Matt Price in the 10th, 12th, and 13th innings. Each time, though, the Gamecocks and he escaped unharmed.

In the bottom of the 13th, Carolina pulled off the unbelievable finish. Thomas led off with a single, and head coach Ray Tanner put junior outfielder Adam Matthews in to pinch run. Matthews had been limited to only thirty-four games all season by a nagging hamstring injury, but he told his coach he could run.

Junior infielder Peter Mooney laid down a bunt, and the Cavs tried to nail the gimpy Matthews at second, but the throw was wide. Robert Beary then got another bunt down, and the Cavs again went for Matthews. Another bad throw bounced away.

Sliding into third base, Matthews had no idea where the ball was, but he could hear third-base coach Chad Holbrook screaming for him to get up and go. He did. "I didn't even look back to see the ball," Matthews said. He scored without a throw.

USC had a classic 3-2 win with an unbelievable finish.

Much of what taxes the limits of our belief system has little effect on our lives. Maybe we don't believe in UFOs, Sasquatch, or the viability of electric cars. A healthy dose of skepticism is a natural defense mechanism that helps protect us in a world that all too often has designs on taking advantage of us.

That's not the case, however, when Jesus and God are part of the mix. Quite unbelievably, we often hear people blithely assert they don't believe in God. Or brazenly declare they believe in God but don't believe Jesus was anything but a good man and a great teacher.

At this point, unbelief becomes dangerous because God doesn't fool around with scoffers. He locks them out of the Promised Land, which isn't a country in the Middle East but Heaven itself.

Given that scenario, it's downright unbelievable that anyone would not believe.

I don't know where to begin.
        -- Ray Tanner, at a loss for words after the 3-2 win over UVa

Perhaps nothing is as unbelievable as that some people insist on not believing in God or his son.

DAY 43

TRUSTWORTHY

Read Psalm 25.

"To you, O lord, I lift up my soul. In you I trust, O my God" (vv. 1-2).

Steve Spurrier trusted his guys to make some plays in the fourth quarter. They did, and the Gamecocks claimed a big win on their way to the SEC East title.

The 17th-ranked Gamecocks celebrated Halloween in 2010 by welcoming Tennessee to Williams-Brice Stadium on Oct. 30. For USC fans, the game at time was a spooky sight.

"That's called football," Spurrier observed after the game as he discussed South Carolina's play. "Some games you make (all the plays), and some games you don't." So the head bird had to trust his players to make some plays when the game was tied at 24 in the fourth quarter and the push to the SEC title game was on the line.

The game appeared well in hand when defensive end Devin Taylor, who had a pair of fumble recoveries, intercepted a Volunteer pass and returned it 24 yards for a touchdown. That gave the Gamecocks a 24-10 lead early in the third quarter.

But Tennessee rallied and tied the game up at 24 with 13:17 on the clock. The Gamecocks needed a play.

They got it only two snaps after the UT touchdown. Quarterback Stephen Garcia hit his sophomore All-American receiver, Alshon Jeffery (See Devotion No. 3.), over the middle, and he

GAMECOCKS

turned on the afterburners, outrunning everybody for a 70-yard score. After that, Spurrier put his trust in freshman running back Marcus Lattimore. He had 84 rushing yards and a TD in the last quarter on his way to 184 yards in his return from an ankle injury.

The Gamecocks responded to their coach's trust with a 38-24 win that kept them ahead of Florida in the SEC East.

The benefits and boons that our modern age has given us have come at a price. One of those costs is the erosion of our trusting nature. Once upon a time in America we encountered strangers or folks we didn't know with a certain openness. Now, wariness is our first response to most situations.

It's not just outlandish claims on TV that have rendered us a nation of skeptics. We have come to accept hucksters as relatively harmless snake-oil salesmen who are just an inevitable feature of a capitalistic economy.

No, the serious damage to our inherent sense of trust has been done in our personal relationships. With much pain, we have learned the truth: Many people just flat can't be trusted.

And then there's God, whom we can trust absolutely. He will not let us down; he is incapable of lying to us; he always delivers on his promises; he is always there when we need him.

In God we can trust. It sounds like a motto we might find on a coin, but it's a statement of absolute truth.

You just keep on playing and you trust your guys can make some plays in the fourth quarter. That's what happened today.
-- Steve Spurrier on the win over Tennessee

We look for the scam before surrendering our trust, but we can trust God without hesitation.

MORE SOUTH CAROLINA

DAY 44

PAY YOUR RESPECTS

Read Mark 8:31-38.

*"He then began to teach them that the Son of Man must
suffer many things and be rejected by the elders, chief
priests and teachers of the law, and that he must be killed"
(v. 31).*

Respect for the opposing team had much to do with the Gamecocks' return to the College World Series in 2012.

After two straight storybook seasons that culminated in the
national titles of 2010 and 2011, South Carolina was a long shot
to even return to Omaha for a third straight time, let alone make
any kind of splash there. That projection was based largely on the
return of only three everyday players -- Evan Marzilli, Christian
Walker, and Adam Matthews -- to the lineup.

Yet, there they were after a 3-2 win over Arkansas, boasting
a 49-18 record and heading into the best-of-three championship
series against Arizona. They beat Arkansas in what had been
typical Gamecock fashion all season, by scratching and clawing.
The winning run came across in the bottom of the seventh
when Matthews drew a two-out, bases-loaded walk that forced
freshman Joey Pankake home. The Gamecocks had forged a 2-2
tie in the fifth when Walker drew a walk with the bases loaded.

Even head coach Ray Tanner struggled for words to provide
some clue as to this team's success. "It's kind of hard to explain,"
he said, pointing to the number of good teams not just in the

GAMECOCKS

College World Series but all across the country, especially in the tough SEC. "Very rarely do we think that we're so much better than the other team," the veteran head coach said.

But that attitude of respect, Tanner said, was a good reason why the Gamecocks of 2012 won so many games. Our guys "respect the game," he said. "They respect their opponents."

As a result, the Gamecocks went out every game and battled their way to one unlikely win after another, in the process gaining their own considerable measure of respect from their opponents.

Rodney Dangerfield made a good living with a comedic repertoire that was basically only countless variations on one punch line: "I don't get no respect." Dangerfield was successful because he struck a chord with his audience. Like the late comedian, we all seek a measure of respect in our lives. We want the respect, the esteem, and the regard we feel we have earned.

But more often than not, we don't get it. Still, we shouldn't feel too badly; we're in good company. In the ultimate example of disrespect, Jesus – the very Son of God -- was treated as the worst type of criminal. He was arrested, bound, scorned, ridiculed, spit upon, tortured, condemned, and executed.

God allowed his son to undergo such treatment because of his high regard and his love for each one of us. We are respected by almighty God! Could anyone else's respect really matter?

Play for your own self-respect and the respect of your teammates.
-- Legendary Vanderbilt football coach Dan McGugin

**You may not get the respect you deserve,
but at least nobody's spitting on you
and driving nails into you as they did to Jesus.**

DAY 45

A HELPING HAND

Read Psalm 121.

"My help comes from the Lord, the maker of heaven and earth" (v. 2).

Michael Roth figured he needed a little help, so as he stepped onto the pitcher's mound, he paused to pray.

Roth is a USC pitching legend. (See Devotion No. 66.) Before that, however, he was a sophomore in 2010 who had not started a game all season and had thrown only 24 innings.

Thus, in Omaha, Roth pitched a combined 2 1/3 innings in the first three games, including 1 1/3 perfect innings in the 12-inning win over Oklahoma on June 24. Even as that game was being played, pitching coach Mark Calvi was trying to decide whom he would start the next day against Clemson. Someone mentioned Roth. Calvi looked over to outfielder Adam Matthews, who was sitting beside him on the team bus, and they both started laughing.

Even Roth thought the idea was ridiculous. When he heard the rumor that he might start, he thought, "That's the biggest joke I've ever heard." But it wasn't a joke. With the Gamecocks one loss away from elimination, "the coaches agonized about the pitching decision, as if they were negotiating a peace treaty." They ultimately decided on Roth.

When Calvi told him, Roth just nodded and kept on watching TV; he didn't believe he would start. "I just figured that, at the last minute, Coach [Ray] Tanner would be like, 'No, no. No, there's no way I'm letting him go out there.'" Reality finally registered for Roth when, just before the team boarded the bus for the ride to the stadium, Tanner asked him how many innings he had in him.

As he took the mound for the biggest game of his life, Roth doffed his cap, held it against his heart, and prayed. He thanked God for the opportunity to pitch and asked for a little help.

He got it, throwing a three-hit, complete-game shutout. The Gamecocks were one win from the national championship series.

As do the Gamecocks in a tightly contested game, we have our ups and downs. Sometimes – often more than once in the journey that is our life – we get to a point when our own resources won't get us through. We need help.

But where to turn? Family and friends? Counselors? Even a pastor? They're certainly better options than the likes of drugs or alcohol. But they're fallible people, and the truth is they sometimes let us down. They simply, for whatever reason, can't or won't provide what we need.

They're derivative anyway; that is, they were all created. The answer for meaningful, life-changing help that will never fail is the Source – Almighty God. God cares for his people, each one of us. The creator of the cosmos cares about you. He knows you by name and knows exactly what's going on in your life. And he has the power and the desire to help – as no one or nothing else can.

I couldn't have pitched that game by myself. I definitely think God was helping me out.

-- Michael Roth on the Clemson game

**"May I help you?" isn't just for a store;
it's a question God will ask if you turn to him.**

DAY 46

JUST PERFECT

Read Matthew 5:43-48.

"Be perfect, therefore, as your heavenly Father is perfect"
(v. 48).

On one glorious afternoon, USC achieved offensive perfection on the football field by scoring every time it had the ball.

South Carolina needed a win over Clemson to finish the 1975 season 7-4 and earn a berth in the Tangerine Bowl. The Gamecocks were favored since the Tigers were enduring a miserable two-win season. And they were confident. Senior quarterback Jeff Grantz was so confident that the day before the game he made a ridiculous promise to calm the nerves of a Gamecock fan. Grantz said USC would score every time it got the ball. Then the team went out and delivered perfection.

South Carolina blasted Clemson 56-20. The Gamecocks rolled up 626 total yards with Clarence Williams rushing for 160 yards and Grantz another 122. He completed only nine of twelve passes, but five of them went for touchdowns. The team's leading receiver, Philip Logan, had two six-point catches with Kevin Long, Randy Chastain, and Stevie Stephens hauling in the other three scores.

As Grantz had promised, the Gamecocks scored every time they got the football -- and it wasn't field goals either. It was touchdowns. "I just kept looking up at the scoreboard and going, 'Man, this is an awesome way to go out,'" Grantz said.

South Carolina led 35-6 at the break. As if to insult the Tigers, the last TD of the half came on a play Grantz drew up in the dirt with Logan and head coach Jim Carlen.

The game's final touchdown came on a 20-yard pass with 54 seconds left, leading many Tiger fans to grouse about running up the score. "What do you do? Kick a field goal?" Grantz asked. "It was my last game. I wasn't going to stand there and take a knee."

With that pass, Grantz and his teammates achieved perfection.

Nobody's perfect; we all make mistakes every day. We botch our personal relationships; at work we seek competence, not perfection. To insist upon personal or professional perfection in our lives is to establish an impossibly high standard that will eventually destroy us physically, emotionally, and mentally.

Yet that is exactly the standard God sets for us. Our love is to be perfect, never ceasing, never failing, never qualified – just the way God loves us. And Jesus didn't limit his command to only preachers and goody-two-shoes types. All of his disciples are to be perfect as they navigate their way through the world's ambiguous definition and understanding of love.

But that's impossible! Well, not necessarily, if to love perfectly is to serve God wholeheartedly and to follow Jesus with single-minded devotion. Anyhow, in his perfect love for us, God makes allowance for our imperfect love and the consequences of it in the perfection of Jesus.

It's execution and perfection. That day was something to see.
-- USC center Mike McCabe on the '75 Clemson game

In his perfect love for us, God provides a way
for us to escape the consequences
of our imperfect love for him: Jesus.

DAY 47

THE OUTER LIMITS

Read Genesis 18:1-15.

"Is anything too hard for the Lord?" (v. 14a)

Jake Williams just didn't possess the ability to make the play that would save the Gamecocks in the College World Series -- or so the critics said. Good thing he didn't pay any attention to them.

Williams knew the assessment of his baseball talents: "Good defense, good bat, weak arm." As an outfielder, he could track down a fly ball, but his arm was "too soft, too erratic, to be counted on" to throw runners out consistently. Williams heard the talk but didn't agree with it. "I sort of think I have a sneaky arm," he said. "When I need to make the throws, I'll make the throws."

A junior, Williams hit .268 with ten home runs and 38 RBIs in 2011. But it was with one throw -- of all things -- that Williams "went from being an OK outfielder to a USC legend" when he made what was called "one of the biggest plays in school history."

On June 27, the Gamecocks met the Florida Gators in the open-ing game of the championship round of the 2011 College World Series. In the bottom of the tenth, the Gators had the winning run at second base with two outs. A single would win the game; after all, "it was not as if South Carolina had Major League arms in the outfield," especially in left field where Williams stood.

Sure enough, the Gator singled to left. Williams scooped the ball on a hop, "set his feet and launched his whole body into the heave toward the plate." Catcher Robert Beary had to hurry up the third-base line to field the ball, but the improbable throw was close enough that he was able to catch it and tag the runner out.

"That was the best throw he has made since I've known him," said head coach Ray Tanner about the play. It was, interestingly enough, Williams' first assist all season.

Kept alive by the throw Williams couldn't make, USC won the game with a run in the eleventh inning.

You've probably never tried a whole bunch of things you've dreamed about doing at one time or another. Like starting your own business. Or going back to school. Campaigning for elected office. Running a marathon.

But what holds you back? Perhaps you hesitate because you see only your limitations, both those you've imposed on yourself and those of which others constantly remind you. But maybe as Jake Williams did, it's time you ignored what everybody says. Maybe it's time to see yourself the way God does.

God sees you as you are and also as you can be. In God's eyes, your possibilities are limitless. To realize those latent possibilities, however, you must depend upon God for direction, guidance, and strength. While you may quail in the face of the challenge that lies before you, nothing is too hard for the Lord.

You can free yourself from that which blights your dreams by depending not on yourself but on God.

Jake couldn't throw the ball twenty yards, and he makes the throw of his life against Florida.

-- Jackie Bradley, Jr.

**Pray like everything depends upon God;
work like everything depends upon you.**

DAY 48

CHEERS

Read Matthew 21:1-11.

"The crowds that went ahead of him and those that followed shouted" (v. 9).

The cheers continued for the 2010 USC baseball team long after they had won the national title.

The cheering, screaming, and hollering began in earnest on June 29 the moment junior outfielder Whit Merrifield's single chased Scott Wingo home for the deciding run against UCLA. The cheers got louder when some 13,000 enthusiastic fans welcomed the national champions home at Colonial Life Arena the next day. (See Devotion No. 79.) Those cheers swelled even more during the parade of champions when about 40,000 Gamecock fans and followers lined both sides of Main Street.

But the cheering wasn't over. Indeed, it hadn't even reached its maximum decibel level. That happened twice.

The first din came before the opening game of the 2010 football season. On Thursday night, Sept. 2, at head football coach Steve Spurrier's insistence, the national champions were introduced to a raucous and ecstatic full house at Williams-Brice Stadium.

The clamor for the team actually started 25 minutes before the kickoff when the players gathered and began a team chant. The cheering escalated to another level when, before departing the field, they gathered in the corner of the end zone in front of the student section and proceeded to bounce up and down to "Sand-

GAMECOCKS

storm." To no one's surprise, the student section went nuts. "This is awesome," Wingo said. "It shows how great these fans are in Columbia."

But they weren't through. The resounding cheers rose up again on Nov. 6 at halftime of the Arkansas football game when the champions were presented their championship rings. "It was an unbelievable feeling," said associate head coach Chad Holbrook about putting the ring on in front of all those screaming fans.

Chances are you go to work every day, do your job well, and then go home to your family. This country couldn't run without you; you're indispensable to the nation's efficiency. Even so, nobody cheers for you or waves pompoms in your face as they did for the 2010 national champions.

It's just as well, since public opinion is notoriously fickle. Consider what happened to Jesus. When he entered Jerusalem, he was the object of raucous cheering and an impromptu parade. The crowd's adulation reached such a frenzy they tore branches off trees and threw their clothes on the ground.

Five days later the crowd shouted again, only this time they screamed for Jesus' execution.

So don't worry too much about not having your personal set of cheering fans. Remember that you do have one personal cheerleader who will never stop pulling for you: God.

I was just jumping up and down and screaming and just waiting for my teammates to come tackle me.
— *Whit Merrifield after his title-winning hit*

**Just like the sports stars,
you have a personal cheerleader: God.**

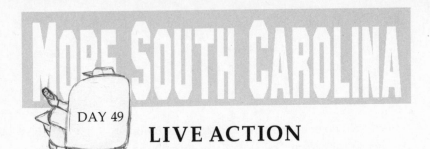
DAY 49

LIVE ACTION

Read James 2:14-26.

"Faith by itself, if it is not accompanied by action, is dead"
(v. 17).

The Gamecock players and coaches had themselves what head coach Steve Spurrier called a "pow-wow talk" about playing better. They did just that, converting the talk into action with a historic victory in their next game.

Three weeks into the 2010 season, South Carolina was 3-0 and had simply demolished Georgia 17-6. The Gamecocks then suffered a disappointing loss to Auburn 35-27 in which they contributed to their own demise by not playing well.

Though perhaps few people at the time appreciated that the Tigers were on their way to the national title, the Gamecocks got together for their "pow-wow talk" after that loss. Spurrier pointed out that they had to put the game behind them and should understand that despite the defeat, all their goals were still there for them to grab. To win the SEC East, though, meant blocking and tackling better than the team had against Auburn.

They needed to start right away. The next opponent after an off week was top-ranked Alabama, and in its long football history, USC had never beaten a No.1-ranked team.

You can't say that anymore. Executing the game plan to perfection, quarterback Stephen Garcia played what was called "the game of his life." The offensive line responded to the "pow-wow

GAMECOCKS

talk" by giving Garcia enough time to complete 17 of 20 passes for 201 yards and three touchdowns. They also opened up holes for running back Marcus Lattimore to roll up 93 yards rushing.

The defense shut down Alabama's running game, including the reigning Heisman-Trophy winner, Mark Ingram. The Tide had only 36 yards rushing on 29 carries. "After missing a load of tackles at Auburn," the Gamecock defenders stopped Alabama's runners dead in their tracks.

So what was the result of all that action on the heels of that little talk? A 35-21 smashing of the top-ranked Crimson Tide.

Talk is cheap. Consider your neighbor or coworker who talks without saying anything, who makes promises she doesn't keep, who brags about his own exploits, who can always tell you how to do something but never shows up for the work. You know that speech without action just doesn't cut it.

That principle applies in the life of a person of faith too. Merely declaring our faith isn't enough, however sincere we may be. It is putting our faith into action that shouts to the world of the depth of our commitment to Christ.

Even Jesus didn't just talk, though he certainly did his share of preaching and teaching. Rather, his ministry was a virtual whirlwind of activity. As he did, so are we to change the world by doing. Anybody can talk about Jesus, but it is when we act for him that we demonstrate how much we love him.

Jesus Christ is alive; so should our faith in him be.

Don't talk too much or too soon.

-- Bear Bryant

Faith that does not reveal itself in action is dead.

DAY 50

BONE TIRED

Read Matthew 11:27-30.

"Come to me, all you who are weary and burdened, and I will give you rest" (v. 11).

The national champions were tired, as they had a right to be -- at least until head coach Ray Tanner took them on a little detour.

On Tuesday, June 29, 2010, South Carolina's baseball team beat UCLA 2-1 in 11 innings to win the school's first major national championship in more than one hundred years of athletics. The players had spent the entire tournament under the pressure of elimination, since an opening-round loss forced them to win six straight games. After the championship came the celebration.

Thus, the whole bunch was exhausted mentally and physically when they clambered aboard a team bus Wednesday to ride to the airport for the flight home to Columbia. Before the bus pulled away from the hotel, though, Tanner pulled the driver aside and asked him to make a detour. The coach didn't have some tourist attraction in mind; instead, the bus passed by a construction site.

The 2010 College World Series was the last to be played at old Rosenblatt Stadium. In 2011, the series would be held at a new state-of-the-art facility, TD Ameritrade Park. As the bus looped around the work site, Tanner just matter-of-factly remarked that it would be nice to return to Omaha in 2011 and help open up the new ballpark.

The players "quickly went from tired to wired." "Close down

the old stadium, open the new one. Let's do it!" one Gamecock shouted. "We'll be back next year!" another asserted. "Those boys thought they could beat the New York Yankees that morning," observed assistant coach Chad Holbrook.

But they didn't have to. All they had to do to make history by christening the new ballpark as they had shut down the old one was beat the field in 2011. Which, of course, they did.

The everyday struggles and burdens of life beat us down. They may be enormous; they may be trivial with a cumulative effect. But they wear us out, so much so that we've even come up with a name for our exhaustion: chronic fatigue syndrome.

Doctors don't help too much. Sleeping pills can zonk us out; muscle relaxers can dull the weariness. Other than that, it's drag on as usual until we can collapse exhaustedly into bed.

Then along comes Jesus, as usual offering hope and relief for what ails us, though in a totally unexpected way. He says take my yoke. Whoa, there! Isn't a yoke a device for work? Exactly.

The mistake we all too often make lies in trying to do it alone. We rely on ourselves instead of Jesus. If we yoke ourselves to our Lord, the unimaginable, limitless power of almighty God is at our disposal to do the heavy lifting for us.

God's strong shoulders and broad back can handle any burdens we can give him. We just have to let them go.

[The champions] would have stormed off the bus right then and played on that pile of dirt if they could have.
-- Travis Haney on the post-series tour of the construction site

Tired is a way of life only when we fail to accept Jesus' invitation to swap our burden for his.

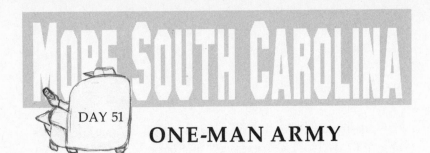

DAY 51

ONE-MAN ARMY

Read Revelation 19:11-21.

*"The rest of them were killed by the sword that came out
of the mouth of the rider on the horse" (v. 21).*

In 2010, Marcus Lattimore was a one-man army against Georgia. In 2011, the sophomore running back waited until the fourth quarter to dominate the Bulldogs.

In one of the SEC's key games of 2011, the Gamecocks went down to Athens for a little get-together on Sept. 10. For a year, Bulldog fans everywhere had had nightmares of what a then-unknown freshman back had done to them in the 2010 game.

In his SEC debut, Lattimore shredded Georgia's defense. He piled up 182 yards rushing on 37 carries and scored the game's only two touchdowns in the 17-6 win that jump-started USC to the championship of the East Division. Georgia simply was no match for Lattimore, who was a one-man army.

Things didn't improve for the Dogs too much in 2011. It just took a little longer for Lattimore to run all over them.

The 2011 matchup between the old foes was the wildest ever. Georgia scored to take a 35-31 lead with 6:28 left in the game. "We weren't going to forget about (Lattimore) even though he was struggling, and we weren't blocking very well," said head coach Steve Spurrier.

Indeed, the Bulldogs wish Spurrier had forgotten. Lattimore took over the game after the kickoff. With 3:48 left, he broke

GAMECOCKS

an arm tackle at the line of scrimmage and streaked down the sideline for a 38-yard romp. He then scored on a 3-yard run with 3:28 on the clock. USC was ahead for good and won 45-42.

In that dominant fourth quarter, Lattimore rushed 13 times for 94 yards. For the night, the one-man USC army had 176 yards on 27 carries. Just for good measure, he had the game-clinching first down that slammed the door on the last Bulldog hopes.

A situation similar to Marcus Lattimore's performances versus UGA will occur when Jesus Christ returns. Our Lord will not come back to us as the meek lamb who was led unprotestingly to slaughter on the cross. Instead, he will be a one-man army, a rider on a white horse who will destroy those forces responsible for disorder and chaos in God's world.

This image of our Jesus as a warrior may shock and discomfort us, but it should also excite and thrill us. It reminds us vividly that God will unleash his awesome power to effect justice and righteousness in a world that persecutes his people and slanders his name. It should also lend us a sense of urgency because the time will pass when decisions for Christ can still be made.

For now, Jesus has an army at his disposal in the billions of Christians around the world. We are Christian soldiers; we have a world to conquer for our Lord – before he returns as a one-man army to finish the job.

It doesn't take a rocket scientist to figure out what the story of the game was. No. 21 for them.
-- UGA head coach Mark Richt after the 2010 USC game

Jesus will return as a one-man army to conquer the forces of evil; for now, we are his army.

DAY 52

RUN FOR IT

Read John 20:1-10.

"Peter and the other disciple started for the tomb. Both were running, but the other disciple outran Peter and reached the tomb first" (vv. 3-4).

The Chanticleers thought they had the game won, and then Christian Walker went for a little run.

On June 13, the Gamecocks met Coastal Carolina in the second game of the super regional with a berth in the 2010 College World Series on the line. As unlikely as it may seem now, Coastal was actually favored, the no.-4 national seed.

The Gamecocks won the first game 4-3, but everything pointed to a third and deciding game when Coastal led 9-7 with two outs and nobody on in the bottom of the eighth inning. The Gamecocks had battled all game long, rallying from deficits of 5-2 and 7-5. This time, though, they were really in a deep hole.

Jackie Bradley, Jr., drew what seemed to be an innocuous walk to bring junior second baseman Adrian Morales to the plate. Head coach Ray Tanner had advised him "to have a quality at-bat here. We can't hit a three-run homer if you're not on base." Morales responded by ripping a double on the first pitch he saw, putting runners at second and third.

That brought up Walker, the team's freshman first baseman. He was thinking home run though he hadn't hit one since May 12. "Everyone was thinking that," Walker said. Tanner had some

GAMECOCKS

advice for his hitter this time, too: "If you see one, crush it."

Walker quickly fell behind 0-2 before he did indeed crush it, sending a hanging slider back where it came from and then some. The ball landed somewhere past the left field fence, and Walker began what he called "one of the better jogs I've taken in my life. I was just making sure I touched all the bases."

Walker's little run covered only 360 feet, but when he finished it, the Gamecocks had a 10-9 lead that stood up. They were still running toward the 2010 national title.

Hit the ground running -- every morning that's what you do as you leave the house and re-enter the rat race. You run errands; you run though a presentation; you give someone a run for his money; you always want to be in the running and never run-of-the-mill.

You're always running toward something, such as your goals, or away from something, such as your past. Many of us spend much of our lives foolhardily attempting to run away from God, the purposes he has for us, and the blessings he is waiting to give us.

No matter how hard or how far you run, though, you can never outrun yourself or God. God keeps pace with you, calling you in the short run to take care of the long run by falling to your knees and running for your life -- to Jesus -- just as Peter and the other disciple ran that first Easter morning.

On your knees, you run all the way to glory.

We thought we had the game won. To lose it [that way] is devastating.
-- Coastal Carolina second baseman Tommy La Stella

You can run to eternity by going to your knees.

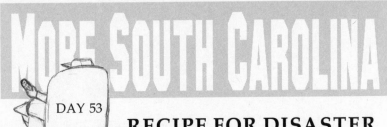
DAY 53

RECIPE FOR DISASTER

Read Luke 21:5-11, 25-28.

"There will be great earthquakes, famines and pestilences in various places, and fearful events and great signs from heaven" (v. 11).

In so many ways, the Gamecocks avoided a seismic disaster in Nashville.

No.-9 USC opened the 2012 football season with a trap game against Vanderbilt on the road rather than with the customary cupcake at home. Therein lay the potential for a disastrous start as a loss would jettison the high ranking and the high expectations the team carried. As *SI* writer Andy Staples put it, "No team ever won a title in week one. But when a team opens with a divisional opponent, it's plenty possible to lose a title in week one."

Moreover, this wasn't your father's Vanderbilt. Rejuvenated by a new head coach, a top-20 recruiting class, and six wins in 2011, the Commodores headed into the game convinced they could play with the big boys. As it turned out, they could.

Vanderbilt went into the fourth quarter with a 13-10 lead, which was disconcerting enough. The real recipe for Gamecock disaster, however, was concocted late in the second quarter; that's when junior quarterback Connor Shaw went to the sideline and then to the dressing room after taking a helmet to his right, throwing shoulder. "I'll be back in there," Shaw replied to the obvious question tailback Marcus Lattimore asked him.

He did come back, and so did Lattimore, returning after missing most of the 2011 season with a knee injury. He rushed for 110 yards and two touchdowns, including the game winner from the 1-yard line.

"It wasn't too pretty, but we'll take the win," Shaw said about the 17-13 victory that avoided a disastrous start. Disaster was also averted in that Shaw's shoulder injury wasn't season-ending.

We live in a world that seems to be either struck by one disaster after another or is the home of several ongoing and seemingly permanent disasters, all of which have consequences on a scale far surpassing a USC loss. Earthquakes virtually obliterate a country; volcanoes erupt and change the climate; children around the world starve to death every day. Floods devastate cities and shatter lives; oil pollutes our oceans and seashores. Can we even count the number of wars that are going on at any one time?

This apparently unending litany of disaster is enough to make us all give up hope. Maybe – but not for the followers of Jesus Christ. The truth is that Jesus' disciples should find reassurance of their ultimate hope in the world's constant disasters because this is exactly what Jesus said would happen.

These disasters indicate that the time of our redemption is drawing near. How near is up to God to decide. Nevertheless, this is a season of hope and great promise for those of the faith.

As they say in golf, never cuss a par.
-- USC associate athletic director Jamie Speronis after the Vandy win

Jesus told us what to do when disaster threatens to overwhelm us and our world: 'Stand up and lift up your heads.'

DAY 54

KNOW-IT-ALLS

Read Matthew 13:10-17.

"The knowledge of the secrets of the kingdom of heaven has been given to you" (v. 11).

Just imagine the kind of season Jadeveon Clowney could have had if he had had time to learn the plays and proper technique.

Clowney arrived in Columbia in 2011 as the nation's top-rated recruit. All that hoopla, however, couldn't completely make up for his inexperience. The defensive end at times needed a veteran to show him where to line up and where to attack. Clowney realized he was somewhat ill-prepared. "I was just tiptoeing out there not knowing what I was supposed to do," he said.

So what was he doing on the field at all? The answer came loud and clear against Georgia. In one of the biggest plays in one of the season's biggest games, Clowney played off a block and closed on the Bulldog quarterback "faster than any 6'6" 256-pounder should." He grabbed the qb's jersey and flung him back toward the goal line. The ball squirted loose, and defensive end Melvin Ingram scooped it up and scored the game-winning touchdown.

Clowney was on the field despite his lack of knowledge because he was too good to keep on the sideline. "If you've got an exceptional player," said defensive line coach Brad Lawing, "to have him over there drinking Gatorade isn't very smart. You get him on the field and have somebody help him through the series."

And that's what the Gamecocks did with Clowney in 2011. He

still had quite a year. His "instincts and freakish physical attributes" led him to five forced fumbles, six quarterback hurries, and eight sacks. He had thirty-six tackles, twelve of them for loss. As defensive tackle Kelcy Quarles put it, "When God made [Clowney], he made a beast."

That "beast" arrived ready to play in 2012, only this time he came armed with knowledge to go with his skills.

We can never know too much. We once thought our formal education ended the day we entered the workplace, but now we participate constantly in training sessions, conferences, and seminars to keep us current whether our expertise lies in medicine or auto mechanics. Many areas require graduate degrees now as we scramble to stay abreast of new discoveries and information. And still we never know it all.

Nowhere, however, is the paucity of our knowledge more stark than it is when we consider God. We will never know even a fraction of all there is to apprehend about the creator of the universe – with one important exception. God has revealed all we need to know about the kingdom of heaven to ensure our salvation. He has opened to us great and eternal secrets.

All we need to know about getting into Heaven is right there in the Bible. With God, ignorance is no excuse and knowledge is salvation.

I didn't know much last season.
> *– Jadeveon Clowney on his freshman year at USC*

When it comes to our salvation, we can indeed know it all because God has revealed to us everything we need to know.

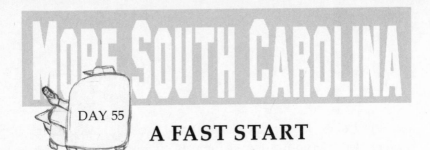
DAY 55

A FAST START

Read Acts 2:40-47.

"Everyone was filled with awe. . . . [They] ate together with glad and sincere hearts, praising God and enjoying the favor of all the people" (vv. 43a, 46b, 47a).

The Gamecocks of 2010 got off to such a slow start that after ten games, head coach Ray Tanner figured the season was shot.

On March 9, as his team fell behind Valparaiso 3-0, Tanner turned to his top assistant coach, Chad Holbrook, and "said something pretty outrageous." He offered his coach a bleak assessment of the rest of the season. "I was due one of these years," he said.

When Tanner spoke of being "due," he was looking back over a decade of success. His teams had made ten straight trips to the NCAA tournament. "There are a lot of outstanding coaches that have had years they'd like to forget," he said. He figured he was looking at what would be his forgettable year.

Thus, a month into the 2010 baseball season, the head Gamecock "had already started to bag the year." He was certainly being "dramatic and prematurely negative," but he had good reason at the time to believe what he sincerely did: that the season was on its way toward being a big disappointment.

His team was 6-4. Against East Carolina, Tanner had watched his squad play with little fire and spunk as they lost two out of three games. The idea struck him that this bunch didn't have "it," that something extra that turned a team into a champion.

GAMECOCKS

Pretty much the whole lot was struggling at the plate. Jackie Bradley, Jr., was out with a broken bone in his right hand. No one had locked down the third starting spot in the pitching rotation. The closer was having trouble nailing games down.

So Tanner watched his team fall behind 3-9 Valparaiso 3-0 and voiced his concern. He never had that thought again. The Gamecocks erupted for ten runs in the third inning and won thirteen straight games and eventually, of course, the national title.

The Gamecocks may not have gotten off to a fast start, but they sure finished strong.

Fast starts are crucial for more than baseball seasons and races. Any time we begin something new, we want to get out of the gate quickly and jump ahead of the pack and stay there.

This is true for our faith life also. For a time after we accepted Christ as our savior, we were on fire with a zeal that wouldn't let us rest, much like the early Christians described in Acts. All too many Christians, however, let that blaze die down until only old ashes remain. We become lukewarm pew sitters.

The Christian life shouldn't be that way. Just because we were tepid yesterday doesn't mean we can't be boiling today. Every day we can turn to God for a spiritual tune-up that will put a new spark in our faith life; with a little tending that spark can soon become a raging fire. Today could be the day our faith life gets off to a fast start – again.

This could be a challenging year. It happens. It happens.
-- Ray Tanner after the 6-4 start in 2010

**Every day offers us yet another chance
to get off to a fast start for Jesus.**

DAY 56

STORY TIME

Read Luke 8:26-39.

*"'Return home and tell how much God has done for you.'
So the man went away and told all over town how much
Jesus had done for him" (v. 39).*

From a Gamecock ordering a hot dog during a game to a player on his way out of the game making a tackle, longtime South Carolina sports information director and author Don Barton can tell some stories.

Barton recalled that during World War II, football personnel varied from game to game. During what was then the Big Thursday game against Clemson in 1943, a new Carolina face entered the game without saying anything. Dom Fusci, a USC Hall of Fame tackle, asked him who he was coming in for. The sub replied, "You." Fusci then asked the newcomer why he hadn't told him. "I thought it might make you mad," he replied.

A somewhat exasperated Fusci had to hurry off the field to prevent a penalty, so he took the quickest route, which just happened to be via the Clemson sideline. There he exchanged pleasantries with legendary Tiger head coach Frank Howard before heading around the end zone for the Gamecock bench. On the way, Fusci spotted a concession stand and stopped and ordered a hot dog. When the concessionaire asked for money, Fusci replied, "Can't you see there ain't no pockets in these pants?"

Barton also recalled that in the 1949 Big Thursday game, USC coach Rex Enright substituted a pair of players, but three came out, including lineman Ed Dew. As he neared the sideline, Dew realized he was the one who was supposed to stay in the game.

Before Dew could turn around and trot back to the line, however, the Tigers ran a sweep toward the Gamecock sideline and appeared headed for a big gain. Dew alertly ran from his spot close to the sideline and tackled the surprised Tiger runner for a loss. He surely must have wondered where in the world Dew came from.

So you weren't a part of some funny moments in South Carolina football history. You nevertheless have a story to tell; it's the story of your life and it's unique. No one else among the billions of people on this planet can tell the same story.

Part of that story is your encounter with Jesus. It's the most important chapter of all, but, strangely enough, believers in Jesus Christ often don't tell it. Otherwise brave and daring Christian men and women who wouldn't think twice of skydiving or whitewater rafting often quail when they are faced with the prospect of speaking about Jesus to someone else. It's the dreaded "W" word: witness. "I just don't know what to say," they sputter.

But witnessing is nothing but telling your story. No one can refute it; no one can claim it isn't true. You don't get into some great theological debate for which you're ill prepared. You just tell the beautiful, awesome story of Jesus and you.

Rex, I discovered where that phantom tackler came from.
-- Frank Howard to Rex Enright the week after the '49 encounter

We all have a story to tell, but the most important part of all is the chapter where we meet Jesus.

MORE SOUTH CAROLINA

DAY 57

CLOTHES HORSE

Read Genesis 37:1-11.

"Israel loved Joseph more than all his children, because he was the son of his old age: and he made him a coat of many colours" (v. 3 KJV).

For the USC-Clemson game of Nov. 27, 2010, Allison Lanning donned what was for her a very peculiar set of clothes. They were heavy on the garnet and black.

At the time, Allison was a sophomore at Clemson and worked as a student assistant in the school's sports information department. Naturally, she was a diehard Clemson fan who customarily wore quite a lot of orange to football games. So why the strange clothes that November night?

It had to do with her brother, Spencer. He was the placekicker and punter and a team captain for the SEC's East Division champs. Allison saw the game as a last chance to support her older brother, who was a senior. So she went all out with the garnet and black and even sat with her parents among the USC partisans.

Allison wasn't alone in her family when it came to supporting Clemson. Even Spencer grew up a rabid Tiger fan. That changed for him, though, when the Gamecocks offered him a chance to join the football team as a preferred walk-on. He eventually won a scholarship and was the team's punter for his last three seasons and the placekicker for his last two. He left Columbia as the most accurate field-goal kicker in school history.

GAMECOCKS

Despite Spencer's success, Allison couldn't force herself to look when he attempted a field goal. "I have to turn around," she said. She learned the outcome from the reaction of the fans around her.

As for that 2010 Clemson game, Spencer had a pretty good night in the 29-7 Carolina romp. To his and his sister's surprise, he missed his first extra point try. After that, though, he booted three field goals with Allison -- in her garnet and black clothes -- turning her eyes away every time.

Contemporary society proclaims that it's all about the clothes. Buy that new suit or dress, those new shoes, and all the sparkling accessories, and you'll be a new person. The changes are only cosmetic, though; under those clothes, you're the same person. Consider Joseph, for instance, prancing about in his pretty new clothes; he was still a spoiled little tattletale whom his brothers detested enough to sell into slavery.

Jesus never taught that we should run around half-naked or wear only second-hand clothes from the local mission. He did warn us, though, against making consumer items such as clothes a priority in our lives. A follower of Christ seeks to emulate Jesus not through material, superficial means such as wearing special clothing like a robe and sandals. Rather, the true disciple desires to match Jesus' inner beauty and serenity -- whether the clothes the Christian wears are the sables of a king or the rags of a pauper.

I have the rest of my life to be a Clemson fan and wear orange. This is my chance to be a Gamecock and support Spencer.
-- Allison Lanning on wearing garnet and black

Where Jesus is concerned,
clothes don't make the person; faith does.

DAY 58

WHO CARES?

Read Psalm 90.

"Teach us to number our days aright, that we may gain a heart of wisdom" (v. 12).

For some college baseball players, the game they play practically every day for four years or so becomes such a routine part of their life that they take it for granted. Not Brady Thomas.

Thomas was a key component of the Gamecocks' run to the 2010 national title. He was second on the team in hitting -- behind Jackie Bradley, Jr. -- with a .331 average and second on the team behind Adrian Morales with thirteen doubles. He hit .381 in the College World Series and was named to the All-Tournament team.

Thomas' college career apparently ended with the 2010 season, but he hoped otherwise. He had played two seasons at FSU before transferring to Columbia. As a sophomore in Tallahassee in 2007, he played in 21 games. The key to his hopes for a 2011 season lay in the 2006 season during which he contracted ulcerative colitis. He played in only nine games, getting only seven at-bats. Thus, he appealed to the NCAA to be granted a medical redshirt for that lost season; that would allow him a sixth season of eligibility.

As the appeal process lumbered on, Thomas couldn't practice with his teammates. He instituted his own training program, and he was preparing to run the steps at Carolina Stadium one day in early February when coaches Chad Holbrook and Jerry Myers delivered the good news: He had been granted the sixth year.

GAMECOCKS

Thomas made the most of it. The team's starting catcher/designated hitter as well as a team captain, he was named to the CWS All-Tournament Team again. He hit .316 for the season, third best on the team, and was second on the squad with 43 RBIs.

"He sort of personifies what we're all about," said head coach Ray Tanner of the player who never took a single moment of playing college baseball in 2011 for granted.

Our daily lives usually settle into a routine; most of us don't exactly flourish in the midst of constant and ongoing chaos. The danger of such familiarity, however, is that we come to take for granted that which is precious in our lives. Our family members, our health, our friends, the security of our jobs. We may even become careless about them to the point of indifference.

But as Brady Thomas' experience illustrates, we can assume nothing about the permanence of anything in our lives. This includes our salvation, which all too many people take for granted. They assume that just because they know who Jesus is, because they live what the world considers to be a "good" life, and because they attend church now and then, that they are saved.

But salvation comes through a commitment to Jesus, a surrendering of our lives to his control, and a love for him that overwhelms us. Taking Jesus and our salvation for granted is a sure sign that such commitment, surrender, and love are lacking.

I worked hard not to take for granted how blessed I was to walk on any field, much less TD Ameritrade Park [in Omaha].
-- Brady Thomas on being eligible for 2011

**Taking Jesus for granted negates the commitment
to him that is necessary for our salvation.**

DAY 59

STAR POWER

Read Luke 10:1-3, 17-20.

"The Lord appointed seventy-two others and sent them two by two ahead of him to every town and place where he was about to go" (v. 1).

It takes a total team effort to get in this position," declared USC head baseball coach Ray Tanner after the Gamecocks won the 2010 national title. That's certainly true, but in the College World Series, five players emerged as stars.

Sophomore center fielder Jackie Bradley, Jr., won the Most Outstanding Player award for the series. He went 10-for-29, hit two homers, and drove in nine runs. His run-scoring single against Oklahoma in the bottom of the 12th inning rescued the Gamecocks when they were one strike away from elimination.

Senior pitcher Blake Cooper "displayed a heart the size of an Omaha steak" during the series. He started three games, two of them on three days' rest, and threw 300 pitches. He was masterful for eight innings in the 7-1 win over UCLA in the first game of the championship series, allowing only three singles.

Junior outfielder Whit Merrifield "laced the biggest hit in the history of USC baseball." His single to right scored the winning run in the 11th inning of the title-clinching 2-1 win over UCLA.

Sophomore left-hander Michael Roth started the series as a "crafty situational reliever." He left it as "one of the gutsiest big-game starters in recent memory." In fourteen innings at the CWS,

GAMECOCKS

he allowed only two runs on nine hits.

Freshman first-baseman Christian Walker, an all-tournament team selection, went 12-for-29 with two homers and five RBIs. He had the game-winning single against Clemson that propelled the Gamecocks into the championship series.

The South Carolina team won the title, but in the process these five individuals emerged as stars in Omaha.

Baseball teams are like other organizations in that they may have a star but the star would be nothing without the supporting cast. It's the same in a private company, in a government bureaucracy, in a military unit, and just about any other team of people with a common goal.

That includes the team known as a church. It may have its "star" in the preacher, who is – like the quarterback or the company CEO – the most visible representative of the team. Preachers are, after all, God's paid, trained professionals.

But when Jesus rounded up a team of seventy-two folks and sent them out, he didn't have any experienced evangelists or any educated seminary graduates on his payroll. All he had was a bunch of no-names who loved him. Centuries later, nothing has changed. God's church still depends on those whose only pay is the satisfaction of serving and whose only qualification is their abiding love for God. God's church needs you.

As a team, we're just as proud as we can ever be.
– Jackie Bradley, Jr., on the 2010 national title

**Yes, the church needs its professional clergy,
but it also needs those who serve as volunteers
because they love God; the church needs you.**

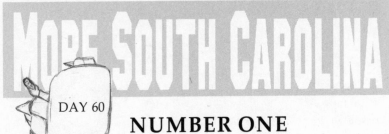

DAY 60

NUMBER ONE

Read Haggai 1:3-11.

"'You expected much, but see, it turned out to be little. Why?' declares the Lord Almighty. 'Because of my house, which remains a ruin, while each of you is busy with his own house'" (v. 9).

As Steve Spurrier leads his Gamecocks through the twists, the turns, and the treachery of a season in the SEC, he always has one priority: the next game.

That's true of the veteran coach even when the next game is the most significant one in school history as it was the week of Nov. 13, 2010. The occasion was a trip down to Gainesville to take on the Florida Gators. On the line were USC's first-ever SEC East Division championship and the school's first-ever trip to the SEC Championship Game. That's all.

But hyping a game never was Spurrier's style. For him, the next game -- whoever the opponent might be and no matter what the situation -- was important simply because it was the next game. Thus, when he spoke to his players on the Friday nights before a Saturday game, he rarely used the occasion to try to motivate or inspire them. Instead, he put his effort into preparing his team.

"We treat [all the games] pretty much the same," he said the week of that trip down to The Swamp to do battle with his alma mater. Thus, to hang around Spurrier the week of that Florida game was to gain no insight into just how really big it was. In fact,

GAMECOCKS

the head coach even admonished quarterback Stephen Garcia for referring to the game as the biggest in Gamecock history.

For Spurrier, the game was important and a priority for the Gamecocks simply because it was the next one. And they won it 36-14, in case anyone's forgotten. After that, as Spurrier pointed out, the priority for the Gamecocks became the Troy University Trojans. USC won that game, too, 69-24.

You have priorities in your life. What is it that you would surrender only with your dying breath? Your family? Every dime you have? Your Gamecock season tickets?

And what about God? What position does God occupy among your priorities? Which of them would you keep even at the cost of denouncing your faith in Jesus Christ?

God doesn't force us to make such unspeakable choices; nevertheless, followers of Jesus Christ often become confused about their priorities because so much in our lives clamors for attention and time. It all seems so worthwhile.

From God's standpoint, though – the only one that matters – if we work for ourselves and ignore our spiritual lives, we will never have enough. Only our deepest needs matter most to God, and these can be met only through putting God first in our lives. To ignore our relationship with God while meeting our physical needs is to travel down the sure road to death and destruction.

God – and God alone – is No. 1.

The next [game] is always the most important because that's the one you have some control over.

-- *Steve Spurrier*

God should always be number one in our lives.

DAY 61

THE SCAPEGOAT

Read Leviticus 16:15-22.

"He is to lay both hands on the head of the live goat and confess over it all the wickedness and rebellion of the Israelites — all their sins — and put them on the goat's head" (v. 21).

Scott Wingo needed only eleven days to go from goat to hero.

Wingo cemented his place in Gamecock lore when he scored the run that won the 2010 national championship. "That's going to live forever," head coach Ray Tanner said of the indelible image the junior second baseman presented when he sprinted home, his helmet flying off, to meet his jubilant teammates after touching home plate.

So much was expected of Wingo in 2011 that he was named a team captain, but he got off to a slow start. As the SEC wars began, his average had dipped to a dismal .205. Even worse, however, had been his "comical-yet-not-funny" missing of the team bus to Greenville for the game of March 8 against Clemson. He had no grand excuse; he had simply overslept.

Tanner placed the fate of his team's goat in the hands of the other two captains, junior pitcher Michael Roth and senior catcher Brady Thomas. Wingo could start the game against Clemson and be suspended for the next five games, or he could sit that night and suffer no further punishment.

Wingo's choice was clear: he wanted to play. The captains felt, though, that losing Wingo for five games was too much, so he sat. Tanner used him as a late defensive replacement in the 5-4 win.

Wingo went from goat to team hero on March 19. With two outs in the bottom of the ninth against Georgia, he slapped an infield bouncer and hustled down the line, sliding headfirst across first base to beat the throw. Adrian Morales scored the winning run.

Wingo was anything but a goat for the rest of the season. He finished that championship year with a .338 average, 81 hits, 103 total bases, and 47 runs scored, all behind only Christian Walker.

A particular type of goat -- a scapegoat – could really be useful. Mess up at work? Bring him in to get chewed out. Make a decision your children don't like? Let him put up with the whining. Forget your anniversary? Call the goat in to grovel and explain.

What a set-up! You don't have to pay the price for your mistakes, your shortcomings, and your failures. You get off scot-free. Exactly the way forgiveness works with Jesus.

Our sins separate us from God because we the unholy can't stand in the presence of the holy God. To remove our guilt, God requires a blood sacrifice. Out of his unimaginable love for us, he provided the sacrifice: his own son. Jesus is the sacrifice made for us; through Jesus and Jesus alone, forgiveness and eternity with God are ours.

It's a bumper sticker, but it's true: We aren't perfect; we're just forgiven.

I felt awful. My last game against Clemson, and I didn't even start.
— Scott Wingo

**For all those times you fail God, you have Jesus
to take the guilt and the blame for you.**

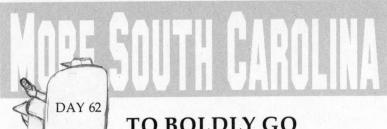

DAY 62

TO BOLDLY GO

Read Acts 4: 1-21.

"Judge for yourselves whether it is right in God's sight to obey you rather than God. For we cannot help speaking about what we have seen and heard" (vv. 19-20).

It was described as "the boldest possible call in such a critical time." It worked, turning the game South Carolina's way.

Against Clemson in Death Valley in 1984, USC trailed 21-3 in the first half. With 42 seconds to go before the break, Scott Hagler kicked a field goal that temporarily made the score 21-6. But the Tigers roughed Hagler up, giving USC a first down.

It apparently didn't help as the Gamecocks wound up facing fourth and four on the Clemson 5 with time running out. The easy call was for the field goal, but head coach Joe Morrison made the bold call. South Carolina was going for it.

But that wasn't all. The easy call was for a pass. But when the play came in, senior receiver Bill Bradshaw's eyes got real big. The Gamecocks were really about to try something bold. The call was a trap handoff to Quinton Lewis, which meant the play would be run right at Clemson's legendary nose guard, William "Refrigerator" Perry.

The bold call worked perfectly. When Perry took a side, center Tommy Garner shoved him out of the way, opening a lane for Lewis. The score cut the lead to 21-10, and the game was never the same again.

GAMECOCKS

Tony Guyton sacked Clemson's quarterback for a safety early in the second half, and Hagler booted another field goal to make it a 21-15 game with seven minutes left.

"We hadn't had a sustained drive all day long," remembered guard Del Wilkes, but the Gamecocks put together an 84-yard drive to win it. Quarterback Mike Hold kept on an option from seven yards out, and Hagler booted the PAT for the 22-21 final.

The game swung on that bold call late in the first half.

To act boldly is to take unconventional action that involves risk as Joe Morrison and his Gamecocks did against Clemson. We all at times in our lives act boldly. When you proposed marriage, for example. Or when you took that new job. We act boldly because we believe the reward justifies the risk.

Why is it then that so many of us who are confident and bold in our professional and personal lives are such timid little things when it comes to our faith life? Why are we so afraid to speak boldly of and act boldly for Jesus? Do we fear offending someone? Are we afraid of rejection? And yet we allegedly serve a Lord who went out of his way to offend the religious authorities and who ultimately was rejected unto death. If anything, Jesus was bold.

Our faith should be burning so strongly in us that we cannot help but live boldly for Jesus. After all, how can we expect Jesus to step boldly forward on judgment day and claim us as his own when we don't claim him as our own now?

We ran a trap and swung the momentum in that game.
-- Quinton Lewis on the bold call before halftime

We serve a Lord bold enough to die for us;
we should at least live boldly for him.

MORE SOUTH CAROLINA

DAY 63

SWEET WORDS

Read Romans 8:31b-39.

"In all these things we are more than conquerors through him who loved us" (v. 37).

Steve Spurrier turned to the best possible source for the affirmation he provided his starting quarterback: the Bible.

When Connor Shaw suffered a right shoulder bruise in 2012's season-opening 17-13 win over Vanderbilt, the quarterbacking duties fell on sophomore Dylan Thompson. He had never started a college game, and like the Gamecock offense in general, had struggled against the Commodores. But he was the choice to start the next weekend against East Carolina as Shaw was still feeling the effects of his injury.

Prior to the game, several receivers stopped by Thompson's hotel room to tell him they knew the team could win with him at the helm. Spurrier also came by to share a Bible verse with his young quarterback, a spiritual affirmation that said God was with him wherever he went. Gamecock fans provided encouragement by sending Thompson messages with Bible verses.

So how did Thompson do against East Carolina? Pretty well, thank you. He completed 21 of 37 passes for 330 yards and three touchdowns in the 48-10 romp. He didn't throw an interception.

Thompson's first completion of the game wound up covering 53 yards to wide receiver Damiere Byrd. Running back Marcus Lattimore scored from the 6 on the next play. An excited Thompson sprinted to the sideline where he danced a jig and jumped up and down a few times.

At one point he even offered a little affirmation to the head man. After he failed to get the clock stopped late in the first half and was greeted with some choice words from Spurrier, Thompson responded by giving his coach a reassuring pat on the back.

After the game, Spurrier in turn affirmed Thompson's play. "Today, he was extremely good" (on just about every play), he said.

You make a key decision. All excited, you tell your best friend or spouse and anxiously await a reaction. "Boy, that was dumb" is the answer you get. A friend's life spirals out of control. Do you pretend you don't know that messed-up person?

Everybody needs affirmation in some degree. That is, we all occasionally need someone to say something positive about us, that we are worth something, and that God loves us.

The follower of Jesus does what our Lord did when he encountered someone whose life was a mess. Rather than seeing what they were, he saw what they could become. Life is hard; it breaks us all to some degree. To be like Jesus, we see past the problems of the broken and the hurting and envision their potential, understanding that not condemning is not condoning.

The Christian's words of affirmation are the greatest, most joyous of all. They constitute a message of victory and triumph from which nothing can separate us or defeat us.

I appreciated the 9 million Bible verses people are sending me.
-- Dylan Thompson on the affirmation he received from fans

The greatest way to affirm lost persons
is to lead them to Christ.

DAY 64

YOUNG BLOOD

Read Jeremiah 1:4-10.

*"The Lord said to me, 'Do not say, 'I am only a child' . . .
for I am with you and will rescue you" (vv. 7a, 8).*

Christian Walker started out young.

Head Gamecock Ray Tanner was obviously more interested in Walker's talent than his youth when he accepted a commitment from him when Walker was still a sophomore in high school. Tanner's faith was rewarded as Walker was rated the 88th best prep prospect in the nation as a senior.

Tanner also felt no hesitation about Walker's youth when he showed up in Columbia. On Feb. 19, 2010, opening day of the season, the head coach's lineup card had the freshman right there in the lineup at third base -- and hitting third. Walker's strong showing at fall practice had convinced Tanner he was ready, no matter how old he was -- or wasn't.

And Walker wasn't really nervous about the whole deal, even though ten of his family members traveled to Columbia for that first game. "A lot of people talked to me about being nervous," he said. "I told them it was more about being anxious to get out on the field and get the season started."

So how did the freshman do in that first game of his collegiate experience? Not too badly. He went 2-for-5 and hit a home run in the 10-3 win. He finished the three-game series 8-for-14 with a double, two homers, five runs scored, and seven RBIs.

GAMECOCKS

From there, Walker just took off, playing like a grizzled veteran all season long. He hit .327 with nine home runs and 51 RBIs. *Baseball America* named him to its Freshman All-America team.

By the postseason, Walker wasn't really a rookie at all, and he proved as much in the Myrtle Beach Super Regional that year. The Gamecocks needed only a win to advance to the College World Series for the first time since 2004, but Coastal Carolina led 9-7 in the bottom of the eighth. The experienced youngster broke their hearts with a three-run homer that sent USC on to Omaha.

While our media do seem obsessed with youth, most aspects of our society value experience and some hard-won battle scars. Life usually requires us to spend time on the bench as a reserve, waiting for our chance to play with the big boys and girls. Unlike Christian Walker at South Carolina, you probably rode the bench in high school waiting for your chance. You entered college as a freshman. You started out in your career at an entry-level position.

Paying your dues is traditional, but that should never stop you from doing something bold and daring right away. Nowhere is this more true than in your faith life.

You may assert that you are too young and too inexperienced to really do anything worthwhile for God. Those are just excuses, however, and God won't pay a lick of attention to them when he issues a call.

After all, the younger you are, the more time you have to serve.

He's very mature, and he doesn't need to be mollycoddled.
-- Ray Tanner on his freshman phenom, Christian Walker

**Youth is no excuse for not serving God;
it just gives you more time.**

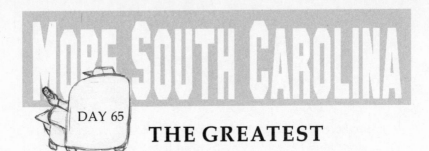

DAY 65

THE GREATEST

Read Mark 9:33-37.

"If anyone wants to be first, he must be the very last, and the servant of all" (v. 35).

Let the record show it for all to see: The 2011 football season was the greatest in Gamecock history.

The celebration of the historic season began in earnest with less than a minute remaining in the 2012 Capital One Bowl when some exuberant Gamecocks gave head coach Steve Spurrier a Gatorade bath. He "was ready to enjoy this one," even though it meant forsaking his tradition that dunkings of the coaches were reserved for games that clinched championships. The occasion was, after all, a 30-13 drubbing of Nebraska that marked the eleventh win of the season, a milestone achieved for the first time since the university fielded its initial football team in 1892.

The Gamecocks finished the 2011 season at 11-2. When the AP released its final poll after the bowl games, USC was No. 9, the program's first-ever finish in the top ten.

Spurrier was well aware of just how momentous the season was. After the win, he gave game balls to every senior and every starter in the bowl game. He also reiterated his promise of a ring to every player to commemorate the season. "It will have a big ol' 11 on it," Spurrier said. "It is neat for this group of seniors to say, 'Hey, I played on the best team ever from South Carolina.' The record speaks for itself as the best team ever."

GAMECOCKS

Some Gamecock fans with long memories may assert that the 1984 Black Magic team that went 10-2 is the greatest ever. Others may argue for the 2001 squad that went 9-3 and beat Ohio State in the Outback Bowl. But the 2011 team's record-setting win total and its ranking in the top ten are hard to argue with.

The team clearly set a new standard both for excellence and for greatness at USC. Echoing that fact, the cheering hadn't even stopped after the bowl game before Spurrier said, "Next year's team, they'll try to win 12 because 11 has already happened."

We all want to be the greatest. The goal for the Gamecocks and their fans every season is a championship. The competition at work is to be the most productive sales person or the Teacher of the Year. In other words, we define being the greatest in terms of the struggle for personal success. It's nothing new; Jesus' disciples saw greatness in the same way.

As Jesus illustrated, though, greatness in the Kingdom of God has nothing to do with the secular world's understanding of success. Rather, the greatest are those who channel their ambition toward the furtherance of Christ's kingdom through love and service, rather than their own advancement, which is a complete reversal of status and values as the world sees them.

After all, who could be greater than the person who has Jesus for a brother and God for a father? And that's every one of us.

We go down in history as the best team to play at Carolina.
-- Safety D.J. Swearinger after the 2012 Capital One Bowl

**To be great for God has nothing to do
with personal advancement and everything to do
with the advancement of Christ's kingdom.**

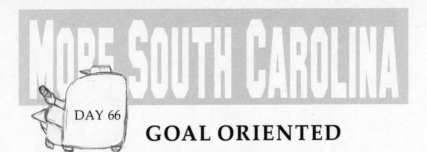

DAY 66

GOAL ORIENTED

Read 1 Peter 1:3-12.

"For you are receiving the goal of your faith, the salvation of your souls" (v. 9).

To be a loving father, to be a loving husband and to chase after Jesus." With that declaration of the goals for his life, one of USC's greatest pitchers conceded that baseball may not be a major part of his future.

Michael Roth completed his storied Gamecock career in 2012 with a 9-1 record and a 2.43 ERA for the national runners-up. He won the President's Award, the most prestigious honor given to a USC student-athlete. He was named the SEC's Athlete of the Year and the Baseball Athlete of the Year. That followed his 14-3 record for the 2011 national champions that garnered him All-American honors and one award as the National Player of the Year.

Roth's performance in the College World Series is the stuff of legend. He holds the all-time record for innings pitched with 60.1; his four wins in Omaha are second all-time only to teammate Matt Price with his five victories. His world series ERA of 1.49 is fifth lowest in history.

Not surprisingly, Roth has dreamed of playing professionally since he first threw a ball, but over the years he has been careful to give himself options other than baseball. That's because despite his wins and his honors, he doesn't throw particularly hard and thus hasn't been regarded as a surefire prospect. When he was a freshman, USC head coach Ray Tanner looked him over on his second day of practice and said, "Roth, you're never gonna touch the mound for me. I don't know why you're throwing."

The Gamecocks were fortunate that Roth has goals outside baseball since they led him to return to Columbia for his senior year to earn a degree in international business. Though he was taken in the ninth round of the June 2012 draft by the Los Angeles Angels, Roth has graduate school as a major goal.

"I wanna do something, come up with something," he said. As he put it, he wants to "change the world."

What are your goals for your life? Have you ever thought them out as Michael Roth has? Or do you just shuffle along living for your paycheck and whatever fun you can manage to find?

Now try this one: What is the goal of your faith life? You go to church to worship God. You read the Bible and study God's word to learn about God and how God wants you to live. But what is it you hope to achieve? What is all that stuff about? For what purpose do you believe that Jesus Christ is God's son?

The answer is actually quite simple: The goal of your faith life is your salvation, and this is the only goal in life that matters. Nothing you will ever seek is as important or as eternal as getting into Heaven and making sure that everybody you know and love will be there too one day.

I know baseball isn't always going to be there.
-- Michael Roth on his life and his goals

The most important goal of your life
is to get to Heaven and to help as many people
as you can to get there one day too.

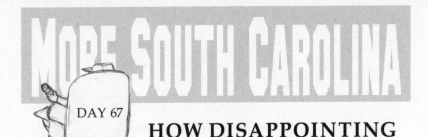

HOW DISAPPOINTING

Read Ezra 3.

"Many of the older priests and Levites and family heads, who had seen the former temple, wept aloud when they saw the foundation of this temple being laid, while many others shouted for joy" (v. 12).

It's easy to forget about it now, but the Gamecocks' 2010 baseball season actually ended in disappointment. The SEC season, that is.

Following a sweep of Arkansas, South Carolina was 42-11 with a 20-7 record in the conference. The final series of the season was at home, a showdown with Florida for the SEC's Eastern Division. The Gators won the series and the title as the Gamecock bats went into cold storage in the first two games, 3-2 and 5-2 losses.

The Gamecocks nevertheless headed into the SEC Tournament confident. The players figured "they were a good team that had a couple of average games." They were in for a real disappointment.

In the opening game against Ole Miss, USC wasted a strong performance from sophomore Nolan Belcher, who had pitched little in the regular season. For the first time in 154 games going back to April 2008, the Gamecocks were shut out. They lost 3-0.

Then, only a solo home run from Brady Thomas kept them from another goose egg against Auburn the next day. The Tigers won 3-1. USC was two-and-through and on its way home, having ended the season by losing four of its last five games.

Head coach Ray Tanner was not too pleased. He decided to use the week he had before regional play began to put some life back into his team. He sent the Gamecocks out onto the practice field five times in three days for a mini-camp on the basics of the game. "We were almost getting treated like Little Leaguers," said senior catcher and team captain Kyle Enders.

Needless to say, it worked. What happened in Omaha erased the disappointing finish from everyone's memory.

We know disappointment. Friends lie to us or betray us; we lose our jobs through no fault of our own; emotional distance grows between us and our children; USC loses; our dreams shatter.

Disappointment occurs when something or somebody fails to meet the expectations we have for them. Since people are people and can't do anything about that, they inevitably will disappoint us. What is absolutely crucial to our day-to-day living, therefore, is not avoiding disappointment but handling it.

One approach is to act as the old people of Israel did at the dedication of the temple. Instead of joyously celebrating the construction of a new place of worship, they wailed and moaned about the lost glories of the old one. They chose disappointment over lost glories rather than the wonders of the present reality.

Disappointment can paralyze us all, but only if we lose sight of an immutable truth: Our lives may not always be what we wish they were, but God is still good to us.

There's nothing disappointing about that.

I was about as unhappy as you could be.
-- Ray Tanner after the 2010 SEC Tournament

Even in disappointing times, we can be confident that God is with us and therefore life is good.

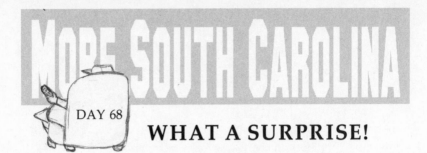

DAY 68

WHAT A SURPRISE!

Read 1 Thessalonians 5:1-11.

*"But you, brothers, are not in darkness so that this day
should surprise you like a thief" (v. 4).*

South Carolina fans were really surprised at the way the 2011
football season started off -- and that wasn't a good thing.

Coming off their SEC East Division title in 2010, the Gamecocks
were highly regarded as the 2011 season kicked off. They were
ranked twelfth in the preseason polls. Thus, fans expected a romp
in the season opener against East Carolina on Sept. 3. After all,
the Pirates weren't exactly SEC-caliber competition. They were
coming off a 6-7 record as a member of Conference USA and had
been dead last in the NCAA in defense the season before.

But to the surprise and consternation of Gamecock fans everywhere, with 9:45 to play in the first half, East Carolina led 17-0 as
the Gamecocks couldn't seem to get out of their own way. At that
point, head coach Steve Spurrier changed up his quarterbacks,
sending in senior Stephen Garcia, who had had his streak of consecutive starts snapped at 28 by sophomore Connor Shaw.

Garcia immediately put points on the board, surprising the
Pirates with a 32-yard option run for a touchdown. Ace Sanders
forced a fumble on the kickoff that Antonio Allen recovered. Less
than two minutes later, Marcus Lattimore scored from the 4.

But East Carolina had one surprise left, an 8-yard TD pass with
three seconds in the half. South Carolina trailed 24-14.

GAMECOCKS

To no one's surprise, however, the Pirates couldn't hold up. They fumbled on their first three possessions of the second half. In only 1:59 according to the clock, the Gamecocks put 21 points on the board to lead 35-24 and take command of the game.

South Carolina went on to win, which wasn't surprising. The final score of 56-37 was something of a surprise, however; the total of 93 points was the third highest in Gamecock history.

Surprise birthday parties are a delight. And what's the fun of opening Christmas presents when we already know what's in them? Some surprises in life provide us with experiences that are both joyful and delightful.

Generally, though, we expend energy and resources to avoid most surprises and the impact they may have upon our lives. We may be surprised by the exact timing of a baby's arrival, but we nevertheless have the bags packed beforehand and the nursery all set for its occupant. Paul used this very image (v. 3) to describe the Day of the Lord, when Jesus will return to claim his own and establish his kingdom. We may be caught by surprise, but we must still be ready.

The consequences of being caught unprepared by a baby's insistence on being born are serious indeed. They pale, however, beside the eternal effects of not being ready when Jesus returns. We prepare ourselves just as Paul told us to (v. 8): We live in faith, hope, and love, ever on the alert for that great, promised day.

Surprise me.
-- Yogi Berra to his wife on where she should bury him

The timing of Jesus' return will be a surprise;
the consequences should not be.

DAY 69

GOOD ADVICE

Read Isaiah 8:11-9:7.

"And he will be called Wonderful Counselor" (v. 9:6b).

Ray Tanner followed some good advice and wound up at South Carolina. He later followed some more good advice and wound up as the most successful coach in school history.

Tanner played baseball for Sam Esposito at NC State. The coach knew the game and brooked no nonsense about it. He was hard-nosed and tough, and Tanner took that style to heart. After seven seasons as an Esposito assistant, Tanner took over the Wolfpack program in 1987. The mentor handed his protege the office keys and a little advice. "Ask for more," he said.

Tanner did. He asked for and received an expanded schedule, but the State brass refused to enlarge Doak Field. Thus, Tanner headed to Columbia in 1996 after USC athletics director Mike Mc-Gee promised to meet just about every one of his demands.

Tanner brought with him the "upfront, confrontational style" he had learned from Esposito. When he gathered his team in The Roost for the first time, he "shut the door and read the riot act to the startled young men." Along the way, though, Tanner sought advice from a former player, Adam Everett, who at the time was in the major leagues. "Have a little fun doing it . . . and let the guys do the same," Everett advised.

Tanner took the advice to heart. He relaxed his rules on facial hair. He played along with the Avatar Spirit Stick in 2010. As his players loosened up, so did Tanner. His style changed from that of a coach to that of a manager, and the results are in the record books: the back-to-back championships of 2010 and 2011, the run to the championship series of 2012, and more than 1,000 wins. In August 2012, he became USC's athletics director.

Like Ray Tanner, we all need a little advice now and then. More often that not, we turn to professional counselors, who are all over the place. Marriage counselors, grief counselors, guidance counselors in our schools, rehabilitation counselors, all sorts of mental health and addiction counselors -- We even have pet counselors. No matter what our situation or problem, we can find plenty of advice for the taking.

The problem, of course, is that we find advice easy to offer but hard to swallow. We also have a rueful tendency to solicit the wrong source for advice, seeking counsel that doesn't really solve our problem but that instead enables us to continue with it.

Our need for outside advice, for an independent perspective on our situation, is actually God-given. God serves many functions in our lives, but one role clearly delineated in his Word is that of Counselor. Jesus himself is described as the "Wonderful Counselor." All the advice we need in our lives is right there for the asking; we don't even have to pay for it except with our faith. God is always there for us: to listen, to lead, and to guide.

Don't make excuses and don't feel sorry for yourself.
-- Advice Ray Tanner received from a high school coach

**We all need and seek advice in our lives,
but the ultimate and most wonderful counselor
is of divine and not human origin.**

DAY 70

A SURE THING

Read Romans 8:28-30.

"We know that in all things God works for the good of those who love him, who have been called according to his purpose" (v. 28).

With the 2012 baseball season approaching, sophomore infielder Erik Payne was a sure thing -- not to start for the Gamecocks. Funny thing about that sure thing.

Payne was not a factor in the drive to the 2011 national title. He was once described as a "tentative freshman who seemed overwhelmed at times." He played in only nine games and had only eight plate appearances with a pair of hits including one double.

Coming off that modest season, Payne didn't figure very prominently in head coach Ray Tanner's plans for 2012. "Absolutely not," Tanner said when asked if he expected Payne to be a starter. So the sophomore was a sure thing to spend a lot of time in 2012 sitting on the Carolina bench as a backup at third base to LB Dantzler, a junior college transfer.

But it turned out that the 2011 season has not been a washout for Payne at all. He had spent it behind fiery third baseman Adrian Morales, the team's leader. (See Devotion No. 25.) More than once, Morales gave the youngster a serious going-over. "He got on me a lot," Payne admitted. He didn't fold; instead he toughened up.

When he was beaten out at third base by Dantzler, Payne didn't get down. Instead, he determined not to give up, and Tanner

GAMECOCKS

noticed the attitude and the hustle.

Thus, when no one stepped forward to claim the starting job at second base, Tanner gave Payne a chance though he had not played the position since the tenth grade. Twenty-five games into the season, Payne started and played so well that the sure bench-warmer became the sure thing at second base. He started thirty games, including those of the College World Series, and gave the national runners-up a solid bat and some reliable defense.

Gamecock baseball games aren't played on paper. That is, the outcome isn't a sure thing. You attend a USC game expecting a win, but you don't know for sure. If you did, why bother to go? Any game worth watching bears an element of uncertainty.

Life doesn't get played on paper either, which means that living, too, comes bearing uncertainty. You never know what's going to happen tomorrow or even an hour from now. Oh, sure, you think you know. Right now you may be certain that you'll be at work Monday morning, that you'll have a job next month, and that you'll be happily and comfortably married to the same spouse five years from now. Life's uncertainties, though, can intervene at any time and disrupt those sure things you count on.

Ironically, while you can't know for sure about this afternoon, you can know for certain about forever. Eternity is a sure thing because it's in God's hands. Your unwavering faith and God's sure promises lock in a certain future for you.

There is nothing in life so uncertain as a sure thing.
-- NHL coach Scotty Bowman

Life is unpredictable, tomorrow is uncertain;
only eternity with or without God is a sure thing.

DAY 71

WHOLEHEARTEDLY

Read 1 Samuel 13:1-14.

"The Lord has sought out a man after his own heart" (v. 14).

The Gamecocks took a shot on a player the coaches knew they would have to teach to pitch. But they liked his heart.

The USC staff wasn't paying any attention to Blake Cooper out of tiny Neese (pop. 313) until pitching coach Mark Calvi saw him throw for a traveling baseball team while he was scouting other players. Jim Toman, Ray Tanner's top assistant coach, had already told Cooper his best shot at college ball lay in the Southern Conference. But Calvi realized that Cooper had something he couldn't teach: He had heart. "For all the things Cooper lacked, and there were plenty physically, drive was not one."

He seemed to be destined to be an immediate star. As a freshman in 2007, Cooper went 7-2, and *Collegiate Baseball* named him a rookie All-America. But he was inconsistent. His ERA was 4.48 that first year. He was 5-6 with a 3.94 ERA as a sophomore in 2008. He had a sterling 9-4 record his junior season, but again his ERA was high at 4.50. Calvi's attitude was "show up to the park and see which Cooper took the mound."

After Cooper's junior season, the heart and drive that had originally caught Calvi's attention manifested itself. He determined that he was done with mediocrity. He didn't want to be good or great; he wanted to be the best.

GAMECOCKS

So he went to work with strength and conditioning coach Billy Anderson and lost twenty pounds before the 2010 season. "He got after it as hard as anybody I've seen," said pitcher Jay Brown. He also added a new pitch to his repertoire, developing a cutter.

Cooper did indeed become the best; he was the ace for the national champions of 2010. He went 13-2 with a 2.76 ERA. In the final start of his career, he allowed one run on only three hits in the 7-1 win over UCLA in the world series championship round.

The kid whose heart and drive compensated for any lack of physical talent was drafted in the twelfth round by the pros.

Blake Cooper just refused to give up, to be beaten by the game he loved. Sometimes, even though we fight with all we have, we lose. Even Cooper and the 2010 Gamecocks lost some games.

At some time, you probably have admitted you were whipped no matter how much it hurt. Always in your life, though, you have known that you would fight for some things with all your heart and never give them up: your family, your country, your friends, your core beliefs.

God should be on that list too. God seeks men and women who will never turn their back on him because they are people after God's own heart. That is, they will never betray God with their unbelief; they will never lose their childlike trust in God; they will never cease to love God with all their heart.

They are lifetime members of God's team; it's a mighty good one to be on, but it takes heart to be there.

He got tired of just doing OK.
-- Mark Calvi on Blake Cooper's determination as a senior

To be on God's team requires a champion's heart.

DAY 72

TOUGH LOVE

Read Mark 10:17-22.

"'One thing you lack,' [Jesus] said. 'Go, sell everything you have and give to the poor, and you will have treasure in heaven. Then come, follow me.' At this the man's face fell. He went away sad" (vv. 21-22).

Rodney Paulk once said he knew right from wrong because "it was instilled in me from when I was a little boy." Some really tough love did the trick.

Paulk's father was an Army Ranger and a drill sergeant. For months on end, he saw "goal-less enlistees," and he vowed not to let his children turn out undisciplined and unqualified academically. The only way he knew to teach them was the way he taught his soldiers. "At first, I wanted them to fear me more than respect me," he said. Thus, in Rodney's early years, dropping for twenty push-ups was the standard punishment around the house.

The drill sergeant softened up some as his sons grew up, but the tough love had its effect on Rodney. He came to Columbia in 2006 to play football, and leaving home did not change him. He didn't curse, he didn't drink any alcohol, he didn't get any tattoos. He called his mom every night at 9. He graduated early with a degree in marine science, a tougher major than those chosen by many of his teammates. He achieved a 3.0 GPA; the only classes he ever missed were when the team was on the road for games.

For his football career at USC, Paulk needed all the focus and determination his dad's tough love had instilled in him. He was a starting linebacker and a freshman All-America in 2006. He was fourth on the team in tackles in 2007. After that, though, injuries pushed him to the sideline and into anonymity in 2008 and 2009.

He played some in 2010 but entered 2011 as an afterthought. As a sixth-year player, though, he emerged as an unsung hero, the third-leading tackler on the history-making squad.

Expect your children to abide by your rules? The immediate reward you receive may be an intense and loud "I hate you," a flounce, and a slammed door. So why do it? Because you're the parent; you love your children, and you want them to become responsible adults. It's tough love.

Jesus also hands out tough love as the story of the young man illustrates. Jesus broke his heart, but the failure was in the young man, who despite his asseverations of devotion, loved his wealth more than he did Jesus.

Jesus is tough on us, too, in that he expects us to follow him no matter what it costs us. A well-executed flounce won't change anything either. As a parent does for his willful children, Jesus knows what is best for us. We'll appreciate that tough love with all our heart and soul on that glorious day when Jesus welcomes us to the place he has prepared for us.

Rodney's a real man. That's the person you want to be like when you grow up.

— USC linebacker Shaq Wilson

**Jesus expects us to do what he has told us to do —
but it's because he loves us and wants the best
for us in life and through eternity.**

FAMILY TRADITION

Read Mark 7:1-7:13.

*"You have let go of the commands of God and are holding
on to the traditions of men" (v. 8).*

The first day Grayson Greiner stepped onto the USC campus as
a student-athlete, he was following a family tradition.

Greiner joined the Gamecocks as a catcher for the 2012 season.
Collegiate Baseball named him to its Freshman All-America Team;
he was also chosen for the SEC All-Freshman Team. He started
fifty-three games for USC, hitting .222 with six homers and thirty-
two RBIs. He was especially strong behind the plate, allowing
only 25 stolen bases in 43 attempts.

But playing for the Gamecocks was nothing new for Greiner's
family. His appearance in a baseball uniform, in fact, completed a
unique family trifecta of the three major collegiate sports.

Thirty-six years before Grayson saw his first action, his father,
Mark, played forward for Frank McGuire on the USC basketball
team (1972-76). Before that, Grayson's grandfather, Bill Killoy, was
a kicker for the Carolina football team from 1947-50.

Grayson was delighted to carry on his family's rather unique
tradition of Gamecock athletics. "It's always been my dream to
play here," he said. As long as he can remember, he has known
of his athletic heritage. "Since I've been little," he said, "I've been
hearing about how my dad played basketball and my granddad
played football here."

GAMECOCKS

The latest Gamecock athlete from the Greiner family had a rather unique physique for a catcher. He was officially listed as standing 6-foot-5 and weighing 215 pounds his freshman season. No doubt he inherited that size from the two men in his family who were Carolina athletes before him.

You encounter traditions practically everywhere in your life. Your workplace may have casual Friday. You family may have a particular way of decorating the Christmas tree, or it may gather to celebrate Easter at a certain family member's home.

Your church probably has traditions also. A particular type of music, for instance. Or how often you celebrate Communion. Or the order of worship.

Jesus knew all about religious tradition; after all, he grew up in the Church. He understood, though, the danger that lay in allowing tradition to become a religion in and of itself, and in his encounter with the Pharisees, Jesus rebuked them for just that.

Obviously Jesus changed everything that the world had ever known about faith. That included the traditions that had gradually arisen to define the way the Jews of his day worshipped. Jesus declared that those who truly worship God do not do so by simply observing various traditions, but instead by establishing a meaningful, deep-seated personal relationship with him.

Tradition in our faith life is useful only when it helps to draw us closer to God.

That's a cool little twist.
-- Mark Greiner on his son's carrying on the family's USC tradition

Religious tradition has value only when it serves to strengthen our relationship with God.

DAY 74

FOUND WANTING

Read Psalm 73:23-28.

*"Whom have I in heaven but you? And earth has nothing
I desire besides you" (v. 25).*

The family tree tattooed on his left arm provided a big hint as to what Stephon Gilmore wanted out of the college he played football for. South Carolina fit the bill perfectly.

Gilmore was once described as "an impact player as soon as he stepped on campus." From 2009-2011, he started at cornerback in all forty games in which he appeared. He was a defensive star for the history-making Gamecock teams of 2010 and 2011. He was first-team All-SEC in 2010 and led the 2011 team in interceptions and pass break-ups. He also made the 2011 Fall SEC Academic Honor Roll and was taken in the first round of the 2012 NFL draft.

Not surprisingly, the recruiting battle among major colleges for Gilmore's talents was intense. It came down, however, to what Gilmore wanted, and he knew exactly what that was.

On Gilmore's left arm is a family tree with seven people on it: his parents and his five siblings. Around the Gilmore house in Rock Hill, organized chaos was the norm what with basketball, football, cheerleading, homework, and supper. One of the rules, though, was that the entire family sat down for dinner on Sunday.

Stephon did his part to contribute to the madness. As his dad noted, his elder son "was always running through the house with a football in his hands." And he was good with that football. As

GAMECOCKS

a freshman quarterback, he ran for a touchdown on his first snap.

When it came down to making a decision about leaving home to play college football, that close-knit family was the decisive factor. Stephon didn't want to leave it. "I didn't want to go too far," he said. "I wanted to stay close to my family."

And so he got what he wanted: South Carolina, close enough that he could still make those Sunday dinners.

What do you want out of life? A loving, caring family such as Stephon Gilmore is blessed with, a home of your own, the respect of those whom you admire? Our heart's desires can elevate us to greatness and goodness, but they can also plunge us into destruction, despair, and evil. Drugs, alcohol, sex, power, worldly success, control over others: Do these desires motivate you?

Desires are not inherently evil or bad for you; after all, God planted the capacity to desire in us. The key is determining which of your heart's desires are healthful and are worth pursuing and which are dangerous and are best avoided.

Not surprisingly, the answer to the dilemma lies with God. You consult the one whose own heart's desire is for what is unequivocally best for you, who is driven only by his unqualified love for you. You match what you want for yourself with what God wants for you. Your deepest heart's desire must be the establishment and maintenance of an intimate relationship with God.

I love my family. I wanted to always stay close to them.
-- Stephon Gilmore on his decision to play for USC

**Whether our desires drive us to greatness
or to destruction is determined by whether
they are also God's desires for our lives.**

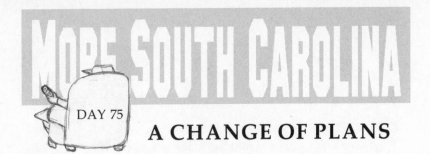
DAY 75

A CHANGE OF PLANS

Read Genesis 18:20-33.

"The Lord said, 'If I find fifty righteous people in the city of Sodom, I will spare the whole place for their sake'" (v. 26).

Mike Matulis thought everything was pretty much planned out -- and then the plans changed

Matulis was a highly recruited offensive tackle, but when he arrived in Columbia in 2011, he found the Gamecocks pretty well stocked with tackles. Kyle Nunn held down the left side, and fellow fifth-year senior Rokevious Watkins was set on the right side of the center. The plan was to redshirt Matulis.

But four games into the season, Nunn went down for the year with a blood clot in his leg. Matulis was called on to start against Auburn, which was a real surprise. "I don't think he ever thought, 'I'm going to play,'" said offensive line coach Shawn Elliott.

Matulis wasn't ready for the sudden change. He was so bad in the Auburn game that he was pulled and replaced by redshirt freshman Cody Gibson, who started the next four games.

"You just can't flip the switch and be ready," Elliott said in defense of his true freshman lineman. Suddenly aware, however, that he might play at any time, Matulis, as Elliott put it, "started paying a lot more attention."

As the season went on and the wins mounted, Spurrier grew restless about the line's pass blocking and suggested another change of plans. He urged Elliott to forget about the redshirt and give Matulis another chance. He started in the crucial game against Florida and played well enough to receive a game ball.

After that, Matulis was in the lineup. *Sporting News* named him a first-team Freshman All-America. With the experience gained from the change in plans in 2011, Matulis entered the 2012 season competing for a starting job at right tackle.

To be unable to adapt to changing circumstances to is stultify and die. It's true of animal life, of business and industry, of the military, of sports teams, of you and your relationships, your job, and your finances.

Changing your plans regularly therefore is rather routine for you. But consider how remarkable it is that the God of the universe may change his mind about something. What in the world could bring that about?

Prayer. Someone -- an old nomad named Abraham or a 21st-century Gamecock fan like you -- talks to God, who listens and considers what is asked of him.

You may feel uncomfortable praying. Maybe you're reluctant and embarrassed; perhaps you feel you're not very good at it. But nobody majors in prayer at school, and as for being reluctant, what have you got to lose? Your answer may even be a change of plans on God's part. Such is the power of prayer.

We don't need to be redshirting guys when we're in the middle of one of the best years we've ever had around here.
-- Steve Spurrier on changing the plans for Mike Matulis

Prayer is so powerful
that it may even change God's mind.

DAY 76

STORM WARNING

Read Luke 12:4-10.

"Whoever acknowledges me before men, the Son of Man will also acknowledge him before the angels of God. But he who disowns me before men will be disowned before the angels of God" (vv. 8-9).

Ray Tanner warned Sean Sullivan to be ready, just in case.

The 10th-ranked Gamecocks were described by one writer as "lifeless" in their series opener against Mississippi State on April 13, 2012. The Bulldogs had knocked out Gamecock ace Michael Roth and led 6-3 with two outs and nobody on base in the bottom of the eighth inning. Turn out the lights; this party was over. Well, not quite.

Freshman Grayson Greiner put a little life into the listless team with a solo home run. "I was just trying to get on base and keep the inning going," he confessed. He did that all right.

Adam Matthews followed with a single, and when sophomore first baseman Brison Celek drilled a double, the Gamecocks were suddenly only one solid hit away from a tie. They got it from an unlikely source.

In the seventh inning, with the uncanny sense of premonition successful coaches sometimes have, Tanner warned little-used junior outfielder Sean Sullivan to be ready. The transfer from Winthrop had batted only twenty times all season and was hitting only .150. Nevertheless, Tanner gave him a heads-up.

Then he called on Sullivan in the eighth inning with the game on the line. Apparently he was ready, lacing a two-strike triple to chase Matthews and Celek home and tie the game. He scored what turned out to be the game-winning run on a wild pitch.

Because Sean Sullivan took advantage of the warning he was given and prepared himself, USC had a 7-6 win.

We spend a great deal of money for equipment and personnel to warn us of impending disasters so we'll be ready. A tornado warning makes us wary. Our nation has a whole system devoted to different levels of warning about the possibility of a terrorist attack. At railroad crossings, signals with their flashing lights and clanging bells warn us of an approaching train.

We are ever on the alert for the warning signs of health problems such as cancer, heart attack, and stroke. Relationship specialists speak of the warning signs of a distressed marriage or a bad relationship.

We heed or ignore these various warnings in direct relation to the sense of urgency they carry for us. No warning, however, should be as urgent for all of us as the one Jesus Christ issued. In his matter-of-fact way, Jesus warned us: Claim him during our life and be claimed as God's own in Heaven; reject him and be banned from Heaven.

We've been warned.

He's been one of the most unselfish players in our dugout the entire season.
-- Ray Tanner on Sean Sullivan, whom he warned to be ready

**Jesus warned us that if we reject him
here on Earth, he will reject us in Heaven.**

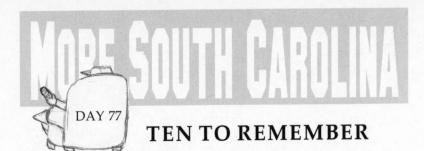

DAY 77

TEN TO REMEMBER

Read Exodus 20:1-17.

"God spoke all these words: 'I am the Lord your God . . . .
You shall have no other gods before me'" (vv. 1, 3).

As the final minutes of 2011 ticked away another magical year for USC baseball, associate head coach Chad Holbrook twittered his top ten moments from the national championship season.

Number 10 on his list was the game of March 18 against Georgia. The Gamecocks were facing an 0-2 start to the SEC season before senior captain Scott Wingo's walk-off infield hit delivered a 2-1 win. No. 9 for the coach was Michael Roth's pitching performance in the 3-1 win over Kentucky on April 1.

Holbrook's no.-8 highlight of the season was the 5-3 win over Vanderbilt on April 17 behind sophomore Matt Price. No. 7 was the 4-3 win over top-ranked Florida in Gainesville on March 27. The coach called winning that road series "an absolutely huge accomplishment."

Holbrook had a tie for his sixth favorite highlight of the season: the 13-4 stomping of Miss. State on April 24 in Starkville (a win that made head coach Ray Tanner so proud he teared up; see Devotion No. 38.) and the 6-3 defeat of Clemson on March 4.

No. 5 on Holbrook's list was the 8-2 win over Connecticut that sent the Gamecocks to Omaha. The fourth best moment was the 3-2 win over Alabama on May 21 that clinched the SEC title.

No. 3 was the 13-inning 3-2 win over top-ranked Virginia in the

College World Series. The second-best moment for the coach was a collection of the double plays in the first game of the championship series against Florida.

And Holbrook's top moment of the season? It was "watching the best center fielder in the country, Jackie Bradley, Jr., tracking the last fly ball," the out that wrapped up the national title.

For Carolina fans, these are indeed ten (or actually eleven) to remember for the ages.

You've got your list and you're ready to go: a gallon of paint and a water hose from the hardware store; chips, peanuts, and sodas from the grocery store for watching tonight's football game with your buddies; the tickets for the band concert. Your list helps you remember.

God also made a list once of things he wanted you to remember; it's called the Ten Commandments. Just as your list reminds you to do something, so does God's list remind you of how you are to act in your dealings with other people and with him. A life dedicated to Jesus is a life devoted to relationships, and God's list emphasizes that the social life and the spiritual life of the faithful cannot be sundered.

God's relationship to you is one of unceasing, unqualified love, and you are to mirror that divine love in your relationships with others. In case you forget, you have a list.

Society today treats the Ten Commandments as if they were the ten suggestions. Never compromise on right or wrong.
-- College baseball coach Gordie Gillespie

God's list is a set of instructions on how you are to conduct yourself with other people and with him.

DAY 78

THE CHALLENGE

Read Matthew 4:12-25.

"Come, follow me," Jesus said (v. 19).

Some of his peers and buddies told him he was crazy to even think about it, but he relished the challenge. So in late 2004, Steve Spurrier took the head coaching job at South Carolina.

After a highly successful 12-year run at Florida, Spurrier left Gainesville for the challenge of the NFL. Two seasons in Washington with the Redskins' owner reminded him of all the reasons why he preferred the college game. But did that mean he had to take on the challenge presented by the program in Columbia?

"Some of my buddies down in Florida said, 'Steve, you're crazy,'" Spurrier recalled. They pointed at the schedule. Its locus in the SEC's East Division meant USC had to play Florida, Georgia, and Tennessee every season. Then there was always Clemson.

Those same naysayers also reminded the coach that in his six seasons at USC, Lou Holtz had had a losing record (33-37). They noted that the program's all-time record was below .500 and that the Gamecocks had played in only nine bowl games before Holtz arrived in Columbia in 1999. All those things were indisputably true.

But while others saw a difficult situation that had worn down some pretty good coaches over the years, Spurrier saw the fun of a challenge. "If you go to a big school and win, you're just doing what somebody else already has done," he said. In effect, USC

GAMECOCKS

offered him the same challenge Florida did; the Gators had never been consistently big winners until Spurrier took over there.

And so, Spurrier met the challenge by building slowly until the Gamecocks won the SEC East in 2010 and eleven games in 2011, along the way going 8-0 against those Four Horsemen on the schedule. "We're not quite there yet," Spurrier said as the 2011 season came to a close. More challenges still lay ahead.

Like the Gamecock athletic teams every time they take the field or the court, we are challenged daily. Life is a testing ground; God intentionally set it up that way. If we are to grow in character, confidence, and perseverance, and if we are to make a difference in the world, we must meet challenges head-on. Few things in life are as boring and as destructive to our sense of self-worth as a job that doesn't offer any challenges.

Our faith life is the same way. The moment we answered Jesus' call to "Come, follow me," we took on the most difficult challenge we will ever face. We are called to be holy by walking in Jesus' footsteps in a world that seeks to render our Lord irrelevant and his influence negligible. The challenge Jesus places before us is to put our faith and our trust in him and not in ourselves or the transitory values of the secular world.

Daily walking in Jesus' footsteps is a challenge, but the path takes us all the way right up to the gates of Heaven – and then right on through.

The possibilities here are just endless.
-- Steve Spurrier on the challenge of coaching at USC

To accept Jesus as Lord is to joyfully take on the challenge of living a holy life in an unholy world.

DAY 79

GOOD JOB

Read Matthew 25:14-30.

"His master replied, 'Well done, good and faithful servant!'" (v. 21)

More than 13,000 Gamecock fans had one thing to say to the 2010 baseball team: "Good job, guys. Well done."

After winning the national title in Omaha Tuesday, the Gamecocks flew home Wednesday, boarded a bus, and went straight to Colonial Life Arena. There, a welcoming party of some 13,000 overjoyed fans filled much of the facility to greet the team. "I was expecting maybe the bottom to be full," said junior outfielder Whit Merrifield, "but what was going on here was just phenomenal." Fans eager to show their appreciation to the champions lined up two and three deep forty minutes before the doors opened. They wore their garnet shirts and caps and cheered as they watched a replay of the dramatic end of the 2-1 clincher against UCLA.

The loudest ovation, however, was reserved for the team, which entered the arena to the familiar, goosebump-raising sounds of "2001." Senior captains Kyle Enders and Jay Brown carried the flashiest hardware in USC athletic history -- the championship trophy -- around for a victory lap. "It's wild in here," commented head coach Ray Tanner.

"This really hadn't sunk in yet until I walked into this place," Enders said about the reception. "It's really amazing."

Other Gamecock coaches were on hand to congratulate Tan-

GAMECOCKS

ner and his boys. They included track coach Curtis Frye, who won the school's only other NCAA title, 2002 in women's track. He said he was thrilled to add Tanner to the club.

USC athletics director Eric Hyman elicited an ear-shattering response from the crowd when he shouted, "I'm going to say it one more time -- national champions." He called what the baseball team did "the dream of dreams."

Everybody agreed: The baseball team had done very well.

Good job. Well done. Way to go.

They are words that make us all swell up a little like a puffer fish and smile no matter how hard we try not to. We may deny it in an honest attempt to be at least reasonably humble, but we all cherish praise. We work hard and we may be well rewarded for it financially, but a cold, hard paycheck is not always enough. We like to be told we're doing something well; we desire to be appreciated.

Nowhere, however, is that affirmation more important than when it comes from God himself. We will all meet God one day, which is intimidating even to consider. How our soul will ring with unspeakable joy on that day of days if we hear God's thundering voice say to us, "Well done, good and faithful servant."

Could anything else really matter other than doing a good job for God?

It was like suddenly by the grace of God, our [Gamecock] sins are forgiven.

-- USC fan Harry Gregory at the Colonial Life Arena

**If we don't do a good job for God in our lives,
all our work elsewhere amounts to nothing.**

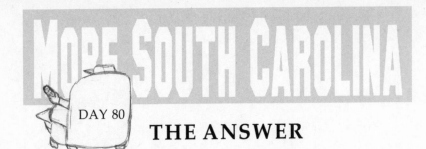

DAY 80

THE ANSWER

Read Colossians 2:2-10.

*"My purpose is that they . . . may know the mystery of
God, namely, Christ, in whom are hidden all the treasures
of wisdom and knowledge" (vv. 2, 3).*

The Kentucky Wildcats had absolutely no answer for anything
the Gamecocks threw at them -- offensively or defensively. The
result was one of the most complete beatdowns in USC and SEC
history.

On Saturday, Oct. 8, on their way to their 11-win season of 2011,
the Gamecocks welcomed the 2-3 Wildcats into what turned out
to be the extremely harsh confines of Williams-Brice Stadium.

With a little help, UK actually got off to a great start when USC
fumbled the opening kickoff. The Cats managed a first down before the "drive" stalled after six plays. A 28-yard field goal jumped
Kentucky into an early 3-0 lead.

But that was it. Even on that first possession, Kentucky had no
answer offensively for the Gamecock defense, but it was to get
worse -- or better, depending upon your perspective. Those six
plays were the last ones the Wildcats ran in South Carolina territory; they never crossed midfield again.

The USC defense was so dominating that Kentucky could muster only 79 yards rushing, but that was an onslaught compared to
their passing game. The Cat quarterbacks actually completed as
many passes to USC players -- four -- as they did to their team-

mates. USC held Kentucky to 17 yards passing, "its stingiest performance in 35 years." UK converted only two of thirteen third-down tries all afternoon.

It might have been a decent ball game had the UK defense had some answers, but they didn't. USC ran off 91 plays for 639 yards.

When the afternoon was over, the only answer that mattered was "54-3." And the question? "What was the final score?"

Experience is essentially the uncovering of answers to some of life's questions, both trivial and profound. You often discover to your dismay that as soon as you learn a few answers, the questions change. Your children get older, your health worsens, your financial situation changes, a South Carolina team struggles unexpectedly -- these are all situations requiring answers to a new set of difficulties.

No answers, though, are more important than the ones you seek in your search for God and the meaning of life because they determine your fate for all eternity. Since a life of faith is a journey and not a destination, the questions do indeed change with your circumstances. The "why" or the "what" you ask God when you're a teenager is vastly different from the quandaries you ponder as an adult.

No matter how you phrase the question, though, the answer inevitably centers on Jesus. And that answer never changes.

Ugly is how you describe it. It was ugly, especially offensively.
-- UK head coach Joker Phillips on the USC game

It doesn't matter what the question is;
if it has to do with life, temporal or eternal,
the answer lies in Jesus.

DAY 81

THE CHICKEN CURSE

Read Jonah 1.

"Tell us, who is responsible for making all this trouble for us? What did you do?" (v. 8a)

South Carolina's three-year run of baseball success from 2010-12 forever broke the spell of The Chicken Curse.

The Curse relates to the school's shortcomings on the athletic fields. Over the decades, many quite logical and identifiable explanations existed for the Gamecocks' failure to bring a championship home to Columbia in football, basketball, or baseball, but notions of a curse persisted. The most common story for the origin of the hex centers on Pitchfork Ben Tillman, a state senator who was instrumental in the founding of Clemson. Upset by the legislature's efforts to prevent Clemson's birth, legend has it Tillman slammed a pitchfork into the ground of the Columbia campus and declared the university to be cursed.

The notion that The Curse existed and that it centered on the school's mascot was so persistent that in 1976 a graduate launched an effort to ditch the Gamecocks. "The Curse says that any team that calls itself a Gamecock will be doomed to a life of athletic mediocrity," wrote Ken Scarlett. "If we change, we can get rid of the Curse forever." The effort didn't get very far.

What finally got rid of The Curse forever was the 2010 baseball team, which still called itself the Gamecocks. When Scott Wingo touched home with the run that beat UCLA, the team didn't just win a national title. It forever "changed the image of USC's athletic department and the attitude of its fans." In other words, the champions exorcised The Chicken Curse.

As if to underscore that The Curse had been laid to rest, the 2010 football team won the championship of the SEC's East Division and then set a school record with 11 wins in 2011. As has been well documented, the baseball team repeated as national champs in 2011. In 2012, USC became only the third school ever to play in the World Series' championship round three straight times.

Curse? What curse?

Some people do feel that they exist under a dark and rainy cloud. Nothing goes right; all their dreams collapse around them; they seem to constantly bring about misery on themselves and also on the ones around them.

Why? Is it really a hex, a jinx?

Nonsense. The Bible provides us an excellent example in Jonah of a person who those around him – namely the sailors on the boat with him -- believed to be a hex. Jonah's life was a mess, but it had nothing to do with a jinx. His life was in shambles because he was disobeying God.

Take a careful look at people you know whose lives are in shambles, including some who profess to believe in God. The key to life lies not just in believing; the responsibility of the believer is to obey God. Problems lie not in hexes but in disobedience.

Well, that curse is gone.
-- USC President Harris Pastides after the 2010 championship

Hexes don't cause us trouble,
but disobedience to God sure does.

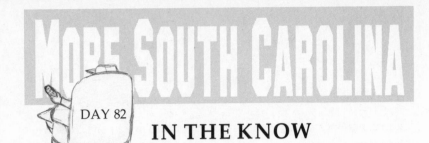
DAY 82

IN THE KNOW

Read John 4:19-26, 39-42.

"They said to the woman, . . . 'Now we have heard for ourselves, and we know that this man really is the Savior of the world'" (v. 42).

Chad Holbrook knew at a glance what was wrong with Jackie Bradley, Jr., and may have saved the star's life. In turn, Bradley knew what the assistant coach was trying to teach him and thus helped make the Gamecocks a baseball powerhouse.

As a sophomore, Bradley was the Most Outstanding Player of the 2010 College World Series after being a Freshman All-America in 2009. At .368, he was by almost forty points the leading hitter for the 2010 champs. He also led the team in RBIs.

In the fall of 2008 in Carolina Stadium's weight room, Bradley approached Holbrook and told the coach he couldn't feel his fingers. Holbrook told him to hold out both arms; "one looked like a twig, the other like a log." The coach had seen a similar situation at North Carolina, so he made a chilling diagnosis on the spot. "Jackie," he said, "you have a blood clot."

Holbrook did his best to remain calm, but he knew that the freshman could, as he put it, "drop dead in a heartbeat." Within an hour, Bradley was in a hospital. Doctors discovered he had an extra rib that forced his blood to flow strangely, a condition he will monitor for the rest of his life, which should be quite lengthy because his assistant coach knew what was wrong.

Conversely, in the fall of 2009, Holbrook worked at consciously tweaking the Gamecocks' approach to hitting. The players were striking out too much, so Holbrook coached them to watch for off-speed pitches to avoid chasing them.

But the juniors and seniors didn't get it because South Carolina was known as a "slugger's paradise," and that was their mentality. "It was like teaching a four corners offense to a basketball team that loved to push the ball up the court," Holbrook said.

But Bradley got it. He knew what Holbrook was doing and was the first to adapt his hitting style. He thus led the way to a change that resulted in three seasons of college baseball history.

Chad Holbrook and Jackie Bradley, Jr., just knew in the same way you know certain things in your life. That your spouse loves you, for instance. That you are good at your job. That tea should be iced and sweetened. You know these things even though no mathematician or philosopher can prove any of this on paper.

It's the same way with faith in Jesus: You just know that he is God's son and the savior of the world. You know it in the same way that you know South Carolina is the only team worth pulling for: with every fiber of your being, with all your heart, your mind, and your soul. You know it despite the mindless babble and the blasphemy of the unbelievers.

You just know, and because you know him, Jesus knows you. And that is all you really need to know.

I pick up stuff real quick.

-- *Jackie Bradley, Jr., to Chad Holbrook*

**A life of faith is lived in certainty and conviction:
You just know you know.**

DAY 83

BEST FRIENDS

Read Ecclesiastes 4:9-12.

"If one falls down, his friend can help him up. But pity the man who falls and has no one to help him up!" (v. 10)

A high-school friend who wound up playing for a rival helped Rokevious Watkins turn his life around.

Watkins arrived in Columbia in 2009 after two seasons at a junior college. He was redshirted, started every game at guard in 2010, and then was first-team All-SEC as a tackle in 2011. He was taken in the fifth round of the 2012 draft by the St. Louis Rams.

Early on, Watkins didn't appear to be headed for such success. He had a tough childhood, living with his mom through most of his middle school years but not getting along with her boyfriend. So, as Watkins described it, he was always "jumping from house to house" in south Atlanta.

He moved in with his dad when his mother moved to Florida, but his father developed throat cancer and had to quit working. Watkins took various jobs at fast-food restaurants. In actuality, he was on the restless, dangerous streets of south Fulton County. "I was just in the streets, point-blank period," he said.

And Watkins wasn't just an observer. "I was a real bad guy then," he admitted. He was both using and dealing drugs and getting into frequent fights at school. Never mind that he and his friend and fellow football player, Eric Berry, had promised each other they would play together in the NFL. The two were so close they had shared the painful ritual of cutting their hands to signify their being blood brothers.

And then one day at school, Berry took his lost friend aside and yelled at him, reminding him of everything he had going for him. "He basically got me straight," Watkins recalled.

Berry went on to star at Tennessee, and when the two teams played in 2009, the rivalry outweighed the friendship for Watkins, at least for one day. "I don't like those guys right now," he said.

Lend him your car or some money. Provide sympathy and comfort when she's down. Lead him out of a bad lifestyle as Eric Berry did for Rokevious Watkins. What wouldn't you do for a friend?

We are wired for friendship. Our psyche drives us to seek both the superficial company of others that casual acquaintance provides and the more meaningful intimacy that true friendship furnishes. We are perhaps at our noblest when we selflessly help a friend.

So if we wouldn't think of turning our back on our friends, why would we not be the truest, most faithful friend of all by sharing with them the gospel of Jesus Christ? Without thinking, we give a friend a ride, but we know someone for years and don't do what we can to save her from eternal damnation.

Apparently, we are quite willing to spend eternity separated from our friends. What kind of lousy friend is that?

He always had my back, no matter what the situation. I think that's really what brought as closer as friends and brothers.
-- Eric Berry on his friend, Rokevious Watkins

**A true friend introduces a friend
to his friend Jesus.**

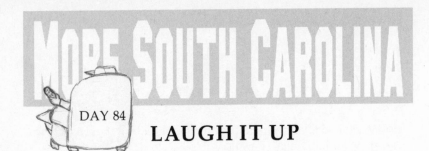

DAY 84

LAUGH IT UP

Read Genesis 21:1-7.

"Sarah said, 'God has brought me laughter, and everyone who hears about this will laugh with me'" (v. 6).

All the two heroes could do was laugh at how improbable the day had been for the Gamecocks.

USC and Alabama engaged in a classic pitcher's duel on Thursday, April 26, 2012. Michael Roth threw nothing but goose-eggs at the Tide, but the Alabama pitcher was better. He had a no-hitter heading into the eighth inning but didn't get to finish. Rain forced the game's postponement until the next day.

The Gamecocks needed only eighteen minutes and one pitch on Friday to notch a win. Senior outfielder Adam Matthews blasted the first pitch he saw for a home run, and Matt Price nailed down the save. Looking squarely at the first no-hitter thrown at them since 1990, the Gamecocks instead had an improbable 1-0 win. "We get one hit . . . and we win a game," head coach Ray Tanner said afterwards. "It's just crazy."

The regularly scheduled game was nothing like the first one, but the outcome was just as unlikely for USC. This one was a slug-fest with Carolina getting home runs from Matthews, Christian Walker, and Grayson Greiner.

The hitting started early on with Alabama leading 7-5 in the fourth before USC rallied with a four-spot and a 9-7 lead. After that, though, Alabama chipped away and took an 11-9 lead into the bottom of the ninth.

The improbable day continued when the Gamecocks rallied for three runs and a 12-11 win. Sean Sullivan's single drove in the game-winner.

On their way to the media room after the game, Matthews and Sullivan joked and laughed about the strange day. "We've played baseball for a long time," Sullivan said, "and really (have) never seen two games like that, especially on one day."

Stand-up comedians and sitcoms are successful because they find humor in the world, and it's often hard for us to do that. "Laughter is foolish," an acerbic Solomon wrote in Ecclesiastes 2:2, his angst overwhelming him because he couldn't find much -- if anything -- in his world to laugh at.

We know how he felt. When we take a good look around at this world we live in, can we really find much to laugh at? It seems everywhere we look we find not just godlessness but ongoing and pervasive tragedy and misery.

Well, we can recognize as Sarah did that in God's innumerable gifts lie irresistible laughter. The great gift of Jesus provides us with more than enough reason to laugh no matter our situation. Through God's grace in Jesus Christ, we can laugh at death, at Satan, at the very gates of hell, at the world's pain.

Because they are of this world, our tears will pass. Because it is of God, our laughter will remain – forever.

Cultivate cheerfulness.

-- *Knute Rockne*

Of the world, sorrow is temporary;
of God, laughter is forever.

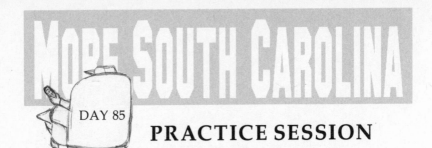

DAY 85

PRACTICE SESSION

Read 2 Peter 1:3-11.

"For if you do these things, you will never fail, and you will receive a rich welcome into the eternal kingdom of our Lord and Savior Jesus Christ" (vv. 10b-11).

His position coach had a rather interesting prediction for Melvin Ingram: He wasn't going to make it as a football player, not because he didn't play well enough, but because he didn't practice hard enough.

Ingram was a can't-miss prospect out of high school. He was so athletic that even as he grew to be 6-1 and 265 pounds, he could still do the back flip his sister taught him when she took gymnastics.

Sure enough, the can't-miss guy started all twelve games at linebacker for the Gamecocks as a freshman in 2007. But trouble came along in 2008 when Ingram missed the entire season after breaking a foot in an accident. When he returned in 2009, things just weren't the same. He couldn't claim a starting job at linebacker and was moved to defensive end. Even there, he was a backup.

Defensive line coach Brad Lawing knew exactly why the projected star wasn't even a starter. So he called Ingram into his office and delivered a simple but scathing message: Ingram was slacking off, especially on the practice field. "You've got tons of ability," Lawing said, "but you don't practice hard." The coach asserted Ingram was even slacking off in the classroom and predicted a bleak future for him when he went back home without a college degree and without any football to play.

Ingram listened. He changed the way he practiced and became a student of the game and a real student in the classroom. As a starter, he led both the East Division champs of 2010 and the 11-win squad of 2011 in sacks. He graduated in December 2011 and was a first-round pick in the 2012 NFL draft.

Imagine a football player who never practices. A play cast that doesn't rehearse. A preacher who never studies the Bible before he delivers a sermon. When the showdown comes, they would be revealed as inept bumblers that merit our disdain.

We practice something so that we will become good at it, so that it becomes so natural that we can pull it off without even having to think about it. Interestingly, if we are to live as Christ wants us to, then we must practice that lifestyle – and showing up at church and sitting stoically on a pew once a week does not constitute practice. To practice successfully, we must participate; we must do repeatedly whatever it is we want to be good at.

We must practice being like Christ by living like Christ every day of our lives. For Christians, practice is a lifestyle that doesn't make perfect -- only Christ is perfect – but it does prepare us for the real thing: the day we meet God face to face and inherit Christ's kingdom.

You play like you practice and you practice like you play.
-- Former Virginia head football coach George Welsh

Practicing the Christian lifestyle doesn't make us perfect, but it does secure us a permanent place beside the perfect one.

DAY 86

BIG DEAL

Read Ephesians 3:1-13.

"His intent was that now, through the church, the
manifold wisdom of God should be made known" (v. 10).

For Whit Merrifield, getting three hits and a win in the College World Series was a pretty big deal. But so was an encounter after the game with a certain well-known blonde.

On June 26, 2010, the Gamecocks edged Clemson 4-3 to earn a berth opposite UCLA in the championship series of the College World Series, which, of course, they won. (See Devotion No. 2.) In the Clemson win, Merrifield, the team's junior right fielder, went 3-for-5 with a double and a triple. For the season, he batted .321 and led the team in hits (95), runs scored (72), and total bases (148) and tied Jackie Bradley, Jr., for the team lead in home runs with 13.

His performance against Clemson earned Merrifield a post-game interview with ESPN's Erin Andrews, whose comments about the injury the junior suffered during the game "might require an increase in cap size." In the eighth inning, Merrifield collided with second-baseman Scott Wingo as they chased a fly ball. Merrifield took the brunt of the encounter with his face.

Andrews "asked me after the game what had happened, and I told her that I just collided and my lip and nose were bleeding," Merrifield recounted. But then Andrews asked the Gamecock if he had lost any teeth, and when he answered that he hadn't, she said, according to Merrifield, "'Well good, because you're too pretty to lose any teeth,' so that was pretty cool."

Writer Eric Boynton noted that "the not-so-smooth Merrifield might have lost the opportunity of a lifetime . . . when his retort to Andrews' compliment was simply, 'Oh, OK.'"

The trip to Omaha turned out to be a pretty big deal for Merrifield and the blondes as he had earlier met country singer and pro dancer Julianne Hough. "As far as the women standpoint, it's been a victory for me this year," he said.

"Big deals" are important components of the unfolding of our lives. Our wedding, childbirth, a new job, a new house, big Gamecock games, even a new car. In many ways, what we regard as a big deal is what shapes not only our lives but our character.

One of the most unfathomable anomalies of faith in America today is that while many people profess to be die-hard Christians, they disdain involvement with a local church. As Paul tells us, however, the Church is a very big deal to God; it is at the heart of his redemptive work; it is a vital part of his eternal purposes.

The Church is no accident of history. It isn't true that Jesus died and all he wound up with for his troubles was the stinking Church. It is no consolation prize.

Rather, the Church is the primary instrument through which God's plan of cosmic and eternal salvation is worked out. And it doesn't get any bigger than that.

I'm fine now, and after the game I got to talk to Erin Andrews and she called me pretty, so it wasn't a total loss.

-- Whit Merrifield

To disdain church involvement is to assert that God doesn't know what he's doing.

DAY 87

THE SYMBOL

Read Mark 15:16-32.

*"Let this Christ, this king of Israel, come down now from
the cross, that we may see and believe" (v. 32a).*

For George Rogers, his Heisman Trophy has become more than
just a coveted prize. It is a symbol he uses to motivate kids.

South Carolina's most famous Gamecock won the trophy as
the country's best college player in 1980 after he led all of college
football in rushing with 1,781 yards. Over the years, the trophy
has always reminded Rogers that the game's most prestigious
award was won by the team and not just by him.

Like many of his teammates, Del Wilkes, a freshman linebacker
on the 1980 team, has always regarded that Heisman Trophy as
something special. "It's still one of the highlights of my career,"
he said, "to say I was the teammate of a Heisman winner."

As the years have passed by, Rogers' perspective on the prize
has changed. When he won it, the trophy served as a symbol for
the pro career that awaited him. Once that career ended, though,
the trophy came to symbolize much more for him. It stands as
both a reminder of the good times and a warning that success
doesn't make anyone immune from life's problems. Rogers has
especially used the trophy to emphasize that message to young
people.

Thus, the trophy hasn't been allowed to rest easy over the fire-
place in Rogers' home. Instead, he has consistently lugged the 25-

lb. symbol of excellence with him to schools and any other place where children gather. "Some of the boys, they can't handle it," he says about the trophy with a smile. "They just keep going 'ooh' and 'aah' even as I start talking."

When he talks, Rogers shares his life experiences as object lessons and his Heisman Trophy as a symbol for them.

Symbols are powerful factors in our lives. Just consider the wellspring of emotions, thoughts, and sensations the passing by of the American flag elicits in many of us. Witness, too, the power of George Rogers' Heisman Trophy to fascinate kids and thus let them hear his message of warning and inspiration.

Some symbols – such as company logos like the swoosh and the golden arches -- are carefully chosen. Others seem to arrive as if by accident or through custom. Christianity's most recognized and beloved symbol is one of the latter. It is the cross, perhaps the most unlikely choice for a symbol in history.

After all, in its time, the cross was a symbol for the ultimate ignominy, the means of execution for the Roman Empire's most scorned criminals and lowlifes. And our lord died on one of them.

Yet, today, for Christians to boldly proclaim their faith for everyone to see, they need only wear a cross. What once symbolized death and despair has become a symbol of hope and love. Such is the transforming power of God through Jesus.

I won the Heisman, but I'm human and I made mistakes. I don't want others to fall through the cracks.

-- *George Rogers*

As he did with the cross, God's love can take our ugly lives and make them beautiful.

DAY 88

NOISEMAKER

Read Psalm 100.

"Shout for joy to the Lord, all the earth!" (v. 1)

Not surprisingly, there was a lot of whooping and hollering in Omaha as the Gamecocks won their second straight national title in 2011. What was surprising was the source of much of that crowd noise.

At the College World Series, the USC fans were loud and vocal "all the way to the finish line of the two-week marathon." But the folks from the Palmetto State who made the long trek to Omaha weren't alone in their noisy enthusiasm; they had support from the locals. Omaha fell in love with the Gamecocks.

One of the more interesting and inexplicable aspects of the College World Series is that Omaha usually picks a favorite. "The city's mysterious selection of favorites has been around for as long as anyone can remember." In other words, as ESPN's Ryan McGee put it, "There's never a plan to the selection process, no organized movement and no declaration from City Hall" that says everyone should pull for this particular team. "It just happens."

In 2011, the city's team of choice was clearly South Carolina. At no time was that more evident than the evening of June 28 when USC beat Florida 5-2 for the title. All game long, the hometown folks "unabashedly cheered for the South Carolina Gamecocks."

Why? USC athletics director Eric Hyman had a possible explanation. "They're just easy to pull for," he said. "They work hard.

GAMECOCKS

They play hard. They're polite. And they're smart."

Lindy Crossman, a student from Bellevue, Neb., who showed up for the game awash in Gamecock gear, had a quite different explanation. "I don't think I could show you where Columbia, S.C., is on a map," she confessed. "But I love this team." Why? "I think they're cute."

As head coach Ray Tanner put it, whatever the reason, "There's something about these guys that Omaha seems to like." What with all the crowd noise, "it felt like a home game."

Whether you're at a Gamecock game live or watching on TV, no doubt you've contributed to the crowd noise generated by thousands of fans or just your buddies. You've probably been known to whoop it up pretty good at some other times in your life, too. The birth of your first child. The concert of your favorite band. That fishing trip when you caught that big ole bass.

But how many times have you ever let loose with a powerful shout to God in celebration of his love for you? Though God certainly deserves it, he doesn't require that you walk around waving pompoms and shouting "Yay, God!" He isn't particularly interested in having you arrested as a public menace.

No, God doesn't seek a big show or a spectacle. A nice little "thank you" is sufficient when it's delivered straight from the heart and comes bearing joy. That kind of noise carries all the way to Heaven; God hears it even if nobody else does.

They really did, didn't they?
-- Ray Tanner on the locals' cheering for his team

The noise God likes to hear is a heartfelt
"thank you," even when it's whispered.

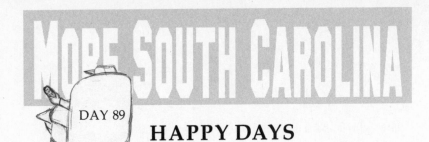

DAY 89

HAPPY DAYS

Read Philippians 4:4-9.

"Rejoice in the Lord always" (v. 4a).

After two straight weeks of being unhappy about the way his team won, Steve Spurrier decided he might as well be happy as long as they walked away winners.

With high hopes and big expectations, the SEC East Division's defending champions opened their 2011 season on Sept. 3 heavily favored against East Carolina. To their fans' amazement and consternation, they promptly fell behind 17-0. Stephen Garcia came off the bench to lead the team on six scoring drives that ultimately turned the game into a 56-37 blowout. (See Devotion No. 68.)

Then on Sept. 10, the Gamecocks won a wild thriller, edging Georgia 45-52. "I've never won a game like this that I can remember," Spurrier said. "Give them credit. [Georgia] outplayed us but somehow or another we won the game."

So were the Gamecocks finished with living on the edge? Apparently not. On Sept. 17, they needed a career game from Marcus Lattimore to come from behind and edge Navy 24-21.

USC appeared to be on the verge of taking control of the game in the third quarter with a drive deep into Navy territory and a 17-14 lead. But the Midshipmen gathered in an interception at the 9 and followed that up with a 91-yard scoring drive. With 3:35 left in the third quarter, Navy led 21-17.

The Gamecocks then simply turned their offense over to Latti-

GAMECOCKS

more. He capped a 79-yard drive with a 7-yard run with 12:45 left to play, and the final score was on the board. The sophomore had a career-best 246 yards and all three touchdowns.

After the game, Spurrier confessed he had been quite unhappy about the first two games but that attitude was behind him. "If you have a big year, you always look back at some of those close ones you win," he said. "We are happy to get this one behind us."

A widespread theology preaches that happiness and prosperity are signs of faithfulness. It's certainly seductive, this notion that with faith comes happiness. But it reduces God to a servant or a vending machine existing only to meet our wishes, coughing up whatever it takes to make us happy. This theology also means that if I am not happy, then God has failed.

Yes, God wants us to be happy. God gave us our life to enjoy; God created this world for us to enjoy; he sure doesn't need it. In God's economy, though, we are to be happy but only with conditions. If it is sin that makes us happy, God doesn't want it for our lives. Moreover, if it is some thing in our lives, some circumstance in our lives, or even some person in our lives that makes us happy, then God is indifferent about it.

God is so good to us that he wants more for us than happiness, which is temporal and worldly. For us, he wants joy, which is eternal and divine and is found only in God through Jesus Christ.

I've lost enough three-pointers in my day to come in here sobbing and crying. I'm happy right now. Happy to get a win.
-- Steve Spurrier after the 24-21 win over Navy

Happiness simply isn't good enough for us because it doesn't depend upon Jesus Christ.

MORE SOUTH CAROLINA

DAY 90

BAGGAGE CHECK

Read Luke 5:17-26.

"Who can forgive sins but God alone?" (v. 21)

The way head coach Ray Tanner packed for the 2012 SEC Tournament illustrated how the Gamecocks' priorities have changed.

The league's postseason soiree took place in Hoover, Ala., from May 22-27. The double-elimination format meant that the Gamecocks could have been there for as few as four days and three nights or as long as six days and five nights. So how do you pack for that? For Tanner, the answer was determined by his priorities as much as by his expectations.

As the veteran head coach boarded the team bus on Monday for the trip west, he confessed that he didn't pack enough clothes to last him through the championship game on Sunday. "But I've got enough (clothes) to get to Thursday," he said. "So, if we win, I can recycle. You can't jinx yourself and pack for a week."

The "jinx" Tanner wouldn't help out by carrying a bulging suitcase to Hoover had to do with USC's recent performance in the tournament. The national champions of 2010 were ignominiously sent back home after two games. The 2011 champs did better but not much; they won their first game before dropping two in a row and packing up for home.

But there was probably more at work in Tanner's suitcase than a "jinx" he didn't really give much credence to. USC had last won the tournament in 2004. Since then, the Gamecocks had gone a miserable 7-14 in Hoover. This was the same program that since 2000 had won more conference games than anybody else. Not to mention, of course, a pair of national titles.

So the point was that the USC baseball program had outgrown the SEC Tournament. The Gamecocks' decisions, including what they packed, were based on securing another trip to the College World Series. As writer Ron Morris put it, Tanner's light suitcase thus illustrated a lack of urgency about the league tournament.

As Ray Tanner demonstrated with what he took to Hoover, the key to successful traveling is taking along only what we need. This applies to our journey through life too. Often, however, we lug along excess baggage: the recriminations we carry from the mistakes we've made, the regrets from the love we failed to give, or the memories of our failures.

Wouldn't it be great if you could just dump all that baggage on the equivalent of an emotional and mental porter, somebody with shoulders broad enough to take the whole load upon himself and set you free from its crushing and oppressive burden? Well, there is somebody, one for whom forgiveness is such a basic part of his nature that he sent his son to us to arrange it.

That somebody is God. He'll take all that baggage – every bit of it -- if you only have faith and trust enough to hand it over to him.

It would be awesome to win out in Hoover, but at the same time, there is more to the postseason than the SEC Tournament.

-- Ray Tanner

One of the most heartbreaking mistakes many people make is believing that the things they've done are too awful for God to forgive.

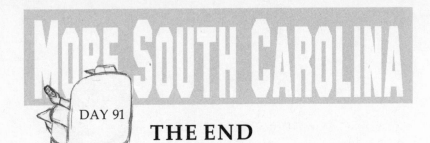
DAY 91

THE END

Read Revelation 22:7-21.

*"I am the Alpha and the Omega, the First and the Last,
the Beginning and the End" (v. 13).*

The end in Columbia for Michael Roth was so good that even the coach whose team he beat had to smile about it.

On June 9, 2012, the Gamecocks hosted the Oklahoma Sooners in the first game of the super regional. The event was significant in that it marked the next step of USC's drive toward a third straight national title. It was special also because Roth made his last appearance on the mound in Carolina Stadium.

Roth was a little-known reliever as a sophomore in 2010 when he threw a three-hitter against Clemson in Omaha. That one win propelled him to the position of staff ace, which he held down quite nicely in 2011 and 2012. He went into the Oklahoma game with a 20-4 mark over the two seasons.

Roth held the Sooners to six hits over 7 2/3 innings, leaving in the eighth after surrendering a two-out hit. In the meantime, third baseman LB Dantzler stroked a double to drive in the first run of the game in the second inning. Erik Payne scored on a wild pitch, and Chase Vergason lifted a sacrifice fly to center to score Dantzler. USC added a pair of runs in the seventh inning on RBI hits from Joey Pankake and Christian Walker. That 5-0 score stood up as the final.

Roth talked his way back to the mound in the eighth inning

GAMECOCKS

after head coach Ray Tanner wanted to sit him down. "You've got ownership here," Tanner told him. When Tanner came to get him, Roth shook hands with his head coach and then came out of the dugout to acknowledge a standing ovation with a tip of his cap.

Roth appreciated the significance of the evening. "I'd be lying to you if I tried to tell you it was just another game for me," he said. "There was something special about tonight." It was so special that OU coach Sunny Golloway had a smile despite the loss. "As a baseball fan and somebody that really loves the game, it was poetic justice," he said about the end of Roth's career at home.

Like Michael Roth's career in Columbia, everything ends. Even the stars have a life cycle, though admittedly it's rather lengthy. Erosion eventually will wear a boulder to a pebble. Life itself is temporary; all living things have a beginning and an end.

Within the framework of our individual lifetimes, we often experience endings. Loved ones, friends, and pets die; relationships fracture; jobs dry up; our health, clothes, lawn mowers, TV sets – they all wear out. Even this world as we know it will end.

But one of the greatest ironies of God's gift of life is that not even death is immune from the great truth of creation that all things must end. That's because through Jesus' life, death, and resurrection, God himself acted to end any power death once had over life. In other words, because of Jesus, the end of life has ended. Eternity is ours for the claiming.

It was classic Roth.
-- USC first baseman Christian Walker on the Oklahoma win

**Everything ends; thanks to Jesus Christ,
so does death.**

THE END   185

NOTES
(by Devotion Day Number)

1   In April, 2003, 5-year-old . . . celebration of the championship. Dirk Chatelain, "Give Up? Boy Didn't, and His Team Hasn't," *Omaha World-Herald*, June 21, 2011, http://omaha.com/article/20110621/CWS/706219822.

1   Several times during the 3-2 . . . "A double play," Charlie replied. Travis Haney, *Gamecock Encore* (Charleston: The History Press, 2012), p. 93.

1   Once we'd get out of a . . . get us some runs.': Haney, *Gamecock Encore*, p. 93.

2   the Bisons "might be the worst team in the entire sixty-four-team field.": Travis Haney, *Gamecock Glory* (Charleston: The History Press, 2011), p. 17.

2   Bucknell led 5-1 in . . . omething had to be done.: Haney, *Gamecock Glory*, pp. 19- 20.

2   the players said and did "stupid stuff all the time.": Haney, *Gamecock Glory*, p. 19.

2   Beary grabbed a bat, a . . . other like, 'No way,'": Haney, *Gamecock Glory*, p. 20.

2   It's pretty dumb when you . . . wasn't that dumb at all.: Haney, *Gamecock Glory*, p. 21.

3   He was committed to basketball . . . better shot with football.": Jordan Conn, "Jeffery's Success Extra Sweet," *SI.com*, July 22, 2011, http://sportsillustrated. cnn.com/2011/writers/jordan_conn/07/22.

3   Jeffery even committed to . . . from across the country.: Conn, "Jeffery's Success Extra Sweet."

3   That was my dream . . . I want to go there.: Conn, "Jeffery's Success Extra Sweet."

4   "arguably the biggest and most significant [win] in program history,": Ron Morris "Something to Celebrate," *The State*, Nov. 15, 2010, p. 15, http://nl.newsbank. com/nl-search/we/Archives?p_action=doc&p_docid=133847CD1F6C11.

4   "It was a good night for . . . really wanted a championship.": Josh Kendall, "Finally, History," *The State*, Nov. 14, 2010, p. 75, http://nl.newsbank.com/nl-search/we/ Archives?p_action=doc&p_docid=1337F533629CA05.

4   "This is one the fans will never forget -- ever,": Kendall, "Finally, History."

4   This is for South Carolina.: Morris, "Something to Celebrate."

5   Marzilli's performance became a . . . complain about the noise,": Neil White, "Sweet Sound of Success," *The State*, Sept. 26, 2010, p. 21, http://nl.newsbank.com/ nl-search/we/Archives?p_action=doc&p_doicid=1327CEA5BA4D.

5   I'm not game for that. . . . 8,000 people and 80,000.: White, "Sweet Sound of Success."

6   The Tiger head coach asked . . . Is this guy joking?'": Haney, *Gamecock Encore*, p. 26.

6   Tanner said it was the only . . . been accused of cheating.: Haney, *Gamecock Encore*, p. 26.

6   The rancor increased with . . . It was a deal.": Haney, *Gamecock Encore*, p. 28.

6   he was offended by . . . happened is appropriate.": Haney, *Gamecock Encore*, p. 29.

6   The players might have been . . . outburst than the win itself.: Haney, *Gamecock Encore*, p. 29.

7   "Connor is used to being pushed.": Josh Kendall, "Wild Week for Shaw's Family," *The State*, Sept. 5, 2010, p. 21, http://nl.newsbank.com/nl-search/we/Archives?p_ action=doc&p_doicid=1320DE168E41A.

7   "As a family, we don't . . . I was really tough on [Connor].": Kendall, "Wild Week for Shaw Family."

7   "I think being a coach's son helped me tremendously.: Kendall, "Wild Week for Shaw Family."

7   "As a dad, I am a blessed man.": Kendall, "Wild Week for Shaw Family."

7   There is a little bit . . . football all the time.: Kendall, "Wild Week for Shaw Family."

8   "You've got a packed . . . nerves get into it.": Ron Morris, "Success Arrives Once Nerves Settle," *The State*, Feb. 18, 2012, p. 23, http://nl.newsbank.com/nl-search/ we/Archives?p_action=doc&p_docid=13CDE241C42D9.

8   "in front of crowds that . . . "It was nerve-wracking.": Morris, "Success Arrives."

8   "that has more letters in its name than it has baseball fans in its stands,": Morris, "Success Arrives."

8   Standing at first, Dantzler . . . "everybody going crazy.": Morris, "Success Arrives."

8   I had the butterflies and I've been doing it a long time.: Morris: "Success Arrives."

9   Sisk "was a fullback at . . . die on the athletic field.: Ron Morris, "A Story Lost in History," *The State*, Sept. 5, 2010, p. 21, http://nl.newsbank.com/nl-search/we/Archives?p_action=doc&p_doicid=1320DE1680E962.

9   I've had a lot of . . . it would be Steve [Sisk].: Morris, "A Story Lost in History."

10   his first staff in 2005 . . . was anybody's guess.: Haney, *Gamecock Glory*, p. 40.

10   "taxing them to the point of breakdown by the postseason.": Haney, *Gamecock Glory*, p. 42.

10   Calvi's frustration reached its . . . pitchers all season long.: Haney, *Gamecock Glory*, p. 41.

10   He wanted to manage . . . over and over again.: Haney, *Gamecock Glory*, p. 42.

10   If you've got them, use them. What are you waiting for?: Haney, *Gamecock Glory*, p. 42.

11   the injury "left many questioning . . . remainder of the year.": Ryan Velasquez, "Wilds Thing," *The Daily Gamecock*, Oct. 29, 2011, http://www.dailygamecock.com/sports/item/2659-gamecocks-wilds-run-past-tennessee-14-3.

11   "I worked hard all . . . "He's a good back,": Velasquez, "Wilds Thing."

11   I just worked hard.: Velasquez, "Wilds Thing."

12   "don't have to be real talkative to be good players,": Josh Kendall, "A Man of Action," *The State*, Sept. 1, 2011, p. 21, http://nl.newsbank.com/nl-search/we/Archives?p_action=doc&p_docid=1397DCD384AA.

12   "preposterously long arms," . . . just like wearing bands,": Kendall, "A Man of Action."

12   "actually talks to me," . . . and have conversations.": Kendall, "A Man of Action."

12   his father is a quiet . . . he grew three more inches,": Kendall, "A Man of Action."

13   He attempted a diving catch . . . pop out of place.: Haney, *Gamecock Encore*, pp. 48-49.

13   In the dugout, he tried . . . worst pain I'd ever felt,": Haney, *Gamecock Encore*, p. 49.

13   "Make it to Omaha and I'll be back.": Haney, *Gamecock Encore*, p. 77.

13   He stubbornly locked his mind . . . to keep him from playing.: Haney, *Gamecock Encore*, p. 51.

13   On June 14, two days before . . . his doctors to play.: Haney, *Gamecock Encore*, p. 76.

13   He looked good during his . . . eighth week after his injury,: Haney, *Gamecock Encore*, p. 77.

13   We thought that was it, yeah. We thought his career was over.: Haney, *Gamecock Encore*, p. 51.

14   Sarge Frye Field was described as "lovable" and "historically charming.": Haney, *Gamecock Glory*, p. 22.

14   Tanner, however, was convinced . . . enthusiasm among USC fans.: Haney, *Gamecock Glory*, p. 22.

14   the coach's "calves were in . . . patience and posturing.: Haney, *Gamecock Glory*, p. 23.

14   The best collegiate only baseball park in the nation.: "Facilities: Carolina Stadium," *South Carolina Gamecocks*, http://www.gamecocksonline.com/facilities/carolina-stadium.html.

15   Gurley failed to qualify . . . the Gamecocks in 2008.: Josh Kendall, "The Long and Winding Road," *The State*, Oct. 30, 2010, p. 47,http://nl.newsbank.com/nl-search/we/Archives?p_action=doc&p_docid=13330517EB099F.

15   "It's an incredible story,": Kendall, "The Long and Winding Road."

15   Hey, I need to get my life together.: Kendall, "The Long and Winding Road."

16 the coaches were quickly smitten with his speed and his intelligence.: Alex Roberts, "South Carolina Gamecock Marty Markett," *Bleacher Report*, April 30, 2012, http://bleacherreport.com/articles/1166532.

16 Markett was the fastest player on the squad.: James Kratch, "Marty Markett Put on Scholarship," *The Daily Gamecock*, Aug. 21, 2011, http://www.dailygamecock.com/sports/item/1728.

16 on August 20, 2011, he . . . 85th and final scholarship.: Kratch, "Marty Markett Put on Scholarship."

16 To receive that scholarship helps out a lot.: Kratch, "Marty Markett Put on Scholarship."

17 sliding into home plate for style points.: Haney, *Gamecock Glory*, p. 96.

17 third-base coach Chad Holbrook . . . his way home from second.: Haney, *Gamecock Glory*, p. 96.

18 "It's a blessing that . . . he does about me,": Josh Kendall, "Ward Takes Charge," *The State*, Dec. 28, 2011, p. 19, http://nl.newsbank.com/nl-search/we/Archives?p_action=doc&p_docid=13BEC29F91901.

18 he stayed up until 5 a.m. studying videos of Nebraska's offense.: Neil White, "Ward Rewards Faith Spurrier Put in Him," *The State*, Jan. 3, 2012, p. 16. http://nl.newsbank.com/nl-search/we/Archives?p_action=doc&p_docid=3C0B4CE2F78E.

18 "This team hasn't panicked . . . to get more physical,: White, "Ward Rewards Faith."

18 "on the backs of its defense.": White, "Ward Rewards Faith."

18 He's the best guy I could hire. That's why I hired him.: Kendall, "Ward Takes Charge."

19 On Big Thursday 1941, the USC . . . wanted this one badly.: Travis Haney and Larry Williams, *Classic Clashes of the Carolina-Clemson Football Rivalry* (Charleston: History Press, 2011), pp. 44-45.

19 Abe Fennell of The State . . . than in a long time.": Haney and Williams, p. 47.

19 "The Gamecocks outrushed, out . . . this was it.": Haney and Williams, p. 47.

19 Rex Enright got a new Cadillac . . . just a few feet of dirt.": Haney and Williams, p. 48.

19 Hope springs eternal . . . . hoping for an upset.: Haney and Williams, p. 47.

20 "The statistics, the percentages of . . . well when you get there.": "Baseball Champs South Carolina Defied Steep Odds," *NPR.org*, June 29, 2011, http://www.npr.org/2011/06/29/137496223.

20 "We're not the most . . . I can't describe it.": "Baseball Champs South Carolina Defied Steep Odds."

20 "despicable, vile, unprincipled scoundrels.": John MacArthur, *Twelve Ordinary Men* (Nashville: W Publishing Group, 2002), p. 152.

20 We're a bunch of average Joes [who] come out and battle.: "Baseball Champs South Carolina Defied Steep Odds."

21 the ball bounced USC's . . . on a routine grounder.: Haney, *Gamecock, Glory*, p. 116.

21 "That didn't work out too well." "No, it didn't,": Neil White, "'Storybook Ending,'": *The State*, July 11, 2010, http://www.thestate.com/2010/07/11/1372586/storybook-ending.html.

21 "The way we're going," . . . drive in those other two.": White, "'Storybook Ending.'"

21 Calvi just looked over . . . for good things to happen,": White, "'Storybook Ending.'"

21 You go through times . . . is going to happen.: White, "'Storybook Ending.'"

22 from feeling pity for the . . . "That's my favorite play,": Josh Kendall, "Tackling a Tough Task," *The State*, Sept. 14, 2010, p. 15, http://nl.newsbank.com/nl-search/we/Archives?p_action=doc&p_docid=323DB285EC56.

22 "Did we run any . . . matter how big they are.": Kendall, "Tackling a Tough Task."

22 I appreciate the sentiment, but don't give us pity.: Stan McNeal, "Cardinal Manager Mike Matheny Doesn't Want Anyone's Pity," *Sporting News*, June 15, 2012, http://aol.sportingnews.com/mlb/story/2012/06-15/st-louis-cardinals-mike-matheny.

23   "there was no question who had carried the Carolina offense": Haney, *Gamecock Encore*, p. 97.

23   Walker swung awkwardly . . . "You better.": Haney, *Gamecock Encore*, p. 97.

23   "It was the worst pain I've . . . for the championship series.: Haney, *Gamecock Encore*, p. 98.

23   Doctors worked with Walker . . . "Are you serious?": Haney, *Gamecock Encore*, p. 99.

23   "I'm not going to go . . . hand's hurting a little bit,": Richard Langford, "South Carolina Baseball's Christian Walker," *BleacherReport.com*, June 3, 2011, http://bleacherreport.com/articles/722716-college-baseball-world-series.

23   Doing everything I can. It's in God's hands at this point.: Richard Langford, "Despite Injury Christian Walker Helps Lead South Carolina Baseball," *BleacherReport.com*, June 3, 2011, http://bleacherreport.com/articles/722716-college-baseball-world-series.

24   "People see us and they . . . "We're real tight.": Neil White, "Quarles Follows Father to USC," *GoGamecocks.com*, Feb. 4, 2010, http://www.thestate.com/2010/02/04/1141154/quarles-follows-father-to-usc.html.

24   often pulling out scrapbooks . . . games at Williams-Brice.: White, "Quarles Follows Father."

24   Kelcy never wavered: White, "Quarles Follows Father."

24   "Oh, man, it's something else," . . . "me and my wife.": Josh Kendall, "Military Stay Suits Quarles," *The State*, Nov. 1, 2011, p. 13, http://nl.newsbank.com/nl-search/we/Archives?p_action=doc&p_docid=13ABF40991ED.

24   He went the long road, but it was good for him.: Kendall, "Military Stay Suits Quarles."

25   "he said words funny; . . . loved him in the spring.": Haney, *Gamecock Glory*, p. 61.

25   "There were guys who . . . they didn't want to,": Haney, *Gamecock Glory*, p. 62.

25   Whit Merrifield said the team . . . he always provided insurance.": Haney, *Gamecock Glory*, p. 63.

25   We couldn't have won without Adrian Morales's leadership.: Haney, *Gamecock Glory*, p. 63.

26   As the Gamecocks trotted to . . . Roth nodded.: Haney, *Gamecock Encore*, p. 81.

26   It's a very unusual feeling . . . and win the first game.: Haney, *Gamecock Encore*, p. 82.

27   "I feel there is a reason . . . he's a rock star,": Andrew Shain, "Spreading Blessings," *The State*, Dec. 24, 2010, p. 19, http://nl.newsbank.com/nl-search/we/Archives?p_action=doc&p_docid=13452603A115AE.

27   Some have the heart . . . has the mouth of Christ.: Shain, "Spreading Blessings."

28   "He hasn't had as many . . . a measure of confidence;: "Chris Dearing, "Belcher Starts Anew," *The State*, April 11, 2012, p. 17, http://nl.newsbank.com/nl-search/we/Archives?p_action=doc&p_docid=13E15A0CDBDA.

29   Holbrook realized that the Bruins . . . gonna do this, Coach!": Haney, *Gamecock Glory*, p. 12.

29   All of those thoughts . . . were going through my head.: Haney, *Gamecock Glory*, p. 12.

30   "That wasn't a punter or . . . "He's a ballplayer,": Matt Connolly, "USC Defensive Lineman Ingram Says 'I Try to Do It All,'" *GoUpstate.com*, Sept. 10, 2011, http://www.goupstate.com/article/20110910/ARTICLES/110919986.

30   Melvin's a great athlete. He can do about anything.: Connolly, "USC Defensive Lineman Ingram."

31   "I told him I could . . . He was, by about a yard.": Bob Juback, "Former Gamecock Remembers 'The Catch,'" *scnow.com*, Sept. 8, 2011, http://www2.scnow.com/sports/2011/sep/08/former-gamecock-remembers-catch-ar-2379353.

31   When he rose from . . . went eerily quiet.: Juback, "Former Gamecock Remembers."

31   "When I go to the . . . catches in Gamecock history.": Juback, "Former

Gamecock Remembers."

31   He was our most . . . he wanted the ball: Juback, "Former Gamecock Remembers."

32   Roth's dad missed both of . . . days to make the trip.: Bard Senkiw, "Roth's Dad Quits
       Job," *Anderson Independent Mail*, June 21, 2011, http://www.independentmail.
       com/news/2011/jun/21.

32   At a family dinner in . . . make it out to Omaha.": "David Roth, Father of South
       Carolina Pitcher Michael Roth, Quits Job," *HuffPost Sports*, June 20, 2011.
       http://www.huffingtonpost.com/2011/06/21/david-roth-quits.

32   My dad's been a huge inspiration for baseball for me: "David Roth," *HuffPost Sports*.

33   "We try to put our players . . . anybody we've got [on the line],": Josh Kendall, "Taylor
       Gladly Drops Back," *The State*, Dec. 28, 2010, p. 13, http://nl.newsbank.com/nl-
       search/we/Archives?p_action=doc&p_docid=134679BB28D8B.

33   He never complained and gave the move his best.: Kendall, "Taylor Gladly Drops
       Back."

33   He's a team player, completely.: Kendall, "Taylor Gladly Drops Back."

34   Gamecock pitching coach Mark . . . Price up for failure.: Haney, *Gamecock Glory*, p. 74.

34   Price was a mystery entering . . . was the team's closer.: Haney, *Gamecock Glory*, p. 75.

34   "This is the worst possible . . . how good he was.: Haney, *Gamecock Glory*, p. 74.

34   Ray Tanner admitted after . . . have been wonderful.: Haney, *Gamecock Glory*, p. 76.

34   That's the worst thing you can do to a kid.: Haney, *Gamecock Glory*, p. 74.

35   defense had struggled "mightily": Neil White, "Defense Shows Its Teeth," *The
       State*, Sept. 25, 2011, p. 60, http://nl.newsbank.com/nl-search/we/Archives?p_
       action=doc&p_docid=139FBEE0281A.

35   the second-fewest yards . . . since at least 1966.: Josh Kendall, "Defense Dominates,"
       The State, Sept. 25, 2011, p. 59. http://nl.newsbank.com/nl-search/we/Archives?
       p_action=doc&p_docid=139FBEE09DD4B.

35   Steve Spurrier apologized to . . . "a putrid offensive performance.": Kendall, "Defense
       Dominates."

35   That was a super defensive game.: Kendall, "Defense Dominates."

36   In May 2011, as his . . . game against the Patriots?: Neil White, "Opening Act Is Classy
       Move," *The State*, April 10, 2012, p. 11, http://nl.newsbank.com/nl-search/we/
       Archives?p_action=doc&p_docid=13E109503590A19.

36   Inabinet had a good reason . . . sold out well in advance.: White, "Opening Act Is
       Classy Move."

36   I did it for the right reasons.: White, "Opening Act Is Classy Move."

37   "my only option at the time.": Darryl Slater, "South Carolina Punter Tyler Hull
       Already Making Impact," *The Post and Courier*, Aug. 15, 2012, http://www.
       postandcourier.com/apps/pbcs.dll/article.

37   Hull looked around and . . . our punter this year.": Slater, "South Carolina Punter
       Tyler Hull."

37   I might as well try . . . see if it works out.: Slater, "South Carolina Punter Tyler Hull."

38   It took doctors a while . . . a pesky hamstring problem.: Haney, *Gamecock Encore*, p. 49.

38   this would not be a . . . we've got and win anyway,": Haney, *Gamecock Encore*, p. 50.

38   a win that "under those . . . bus ride from Mississippi State.": Haney, *Gamecock Encore*,
       p. 50.

38   You've answered the call, and I'm proud of you.: Haney, *Gamecock Encore*, pp. 50-51.

39   "Very few." . . . of experience and intelligence,": Neil White, "Enders Gains Control
       Behind Home Plate," *The State*, March 2, 2010, http://www.thestate.com/
       2010/03/02/1182040/enders-gains-control-behind-home.html.

39   "He handled [Dalles' arrival] with tremendous class and dignity,": White: "Enders
       Gains Control."

39   "It's been more than I expected. It's been a dream come true.": White, "'Our Rock, the
       Unheralded Superstar,'" *National Champions* (Columbia: The State Media Co.,

2010), p. 51.

39 I didn't want to . . . planned it any better.: White, "Enders Gains Control."

40 "the heart of the [USC] offense,": Ron Morris, "Against All Odds," *The State*, Oct. 16, 2011, p. 63. http://nl.newsbank.com/nl-search/we/Archives?p_action=doc&p_docid=13A6A907D783D.

40 he was receiving hugs and . . . a win against Vanderbilt.": Morris, "Against All Odds."

40 Shortly after Shaw spoke . . . the room on crutches,: Morris, "Against All Odds."

40 You think, if enough bad . . . our guys hung in there.: Morris, "Against All Odds."

41 The first person thanked was . . . keep on playing for him.: Travis Haney, "Bayler Teal Was South Carolina's Talisman," *The New York Times*, June 11, 2011, http://www.nytimes.com/2011/06/12/sports/bayler-teal-was-south-carolinas-talisman.html.

41 The players learned minutes . . . weren't going to lose.": Haney, "Bayler Teal."

41 I felt Bayler's hand on my bat.: Haney, "Bayler Teal."

42 "one of the strangest and best games in the history of the College World Series.": Haney, *Gamecock Encore*, p. 88.

42 he told his coach he could run.: Haney, *Gamecock Encore*, p. 92.

42 Sliding into third base, Matthews . . . He scored without a throw.: Haney, *Gamecock Encore*, p. 92.

42 I don't know where to begin.: Haney, *Gamecock Encore*, p. 88.

43 "That's called football," . . . some games you don't.": Josh Kendall, "A Little Bit Rocky," *The State*, Nov. 20, 2010, p. 57, http://nl.newsbank.com/nl-search/we/Archives?p_action=doc&p_docid=1339EEC933DB92.

43 You just keep on p. . . . That's what happened today.: Kendall, "A Little Bit Rocky."

44 "It's kind of hard to . . . "They respect their opponents.": "Gamecocks Headed Back to Title Series," *scnow.com*, June 23, 2012, http://www2.scnow.com/sports/2012/jun/23/5/gamecocks-headed-back-title-series-ar-4024696.

45 Even as the game was . . . they both started laughing.: Haney, *Gamecock Glory*, p. 100.

45 When he heard the . . . negotiating a peace treaty.": Haney, *Gamecock Glory*, p. 100.

45 When Calvi told him, . . . innings he had in him.: Haney, *Gamecock Glory*, p. 101.

45 As he took the mound . . . asked for a little help.: Haney, *Gamecock Glory*, p. 100.

45 I couldn't have pitched that . . . was helping me out.: Haney, *Gamecock Glory*, p. 100.

46 the day before the game . . . every time it got the ball.: Haney and Williams, p. 111.

46 "I just kept looking up at . . . awesome way to go out,'": Haney and Williams, p. 116.

46 the last TD of the half . . . there and take a knee.": Haney and Williams, p. 116.

46 It's execution and perfection. That day was something to see.: Haney and Williams, p. 116.

47 "Good defense, good bat, . . . I'll make the throws.": David Cloninger, "Williams Enters Hero Territory," *GamecockCentral.com*, June 28, 2011, http://southcarolina.rivals.com/content.asp?CID=1235578.

47 "went from being an OK outfielder to a USC legend": Cloninger, "Williams Enters Hero Territory."

47 "one of the biggest plays in school history.": "GamecockCentral Says Jake Williams Won't Be on USC Baseball Team," *TheTandD.com*, Feb. 16, 2012, http://thetandd.com/sports/gamecockcentral-says.

47 "it was not as if . . . arms in the outfield," Haney, *Gamecock Encore*, p. 105.

47 "set his feet and launched . . . to field the ball,: Haney, *Gamecock Encore*, p. 105.

47 "That was the best throw he has made since I've known him,': Cloninger, "Williams Enters Hero Territory."

47 Jake couldn't throw the . . . his life against Florida.: Haney, *Gamecock Encore*, p. 106.

48 at head football coach Steve Spurrier's insistence,: Neil White, "Gamecocks Baseball Team Still Feeling the Love," *The State*, Sept. 3, 2010, p. 26, http://nl.newsbank.com/nl-search/we/Archives?p_action=doc&p_docid=132035109D6C1.

48   The clamor for the team . . . fans are in Columbia.": White, "Gamecocks Baseball Team Still Feeling the Love."

48   "It was an unbelievable feeling,": Neil White, "National Championship Has a Nice Ring to It," *The State*, Nov. 7, 2010, p. 100, http://nl.newsbank.com/nl-search/we/Archives?p_action=doc&p_docid=1335A8A0E37B30.

48   I was just jumping . . . to come tackle me.: Neil White, "History-Making," *thestate.com*, June 30, 2010, http://www.thestate.com/2010/06/30/1356445/usc-national-champions.html.

49   the Gamecocks got together for . . . team had against Auburn.: Ron Morris, "Curse Killers," *The State*, Nov. 20, 2010, p. 48, http://nl.newsbank.com/nl-search/we/Archives?p_action=doc&p_docid=1339EEC921120C.

49   "the game of his life.": Morris, "Curse Killers."

49   "After missing a load of . . . runners dead in their tracks.: Morris, "Curse Killers."

50   Before the bus pulled . . . by a construction site.: Haney, *Gamecock Encore*, p. 13.

50   As the bus looped around . . . open up the new ballpark.: Haney, *Gamecock Encore*, pp. 13-14.

50   The players "quickly went . . . Yankees that morning,": Haney, *Gamecock Encore*, p. 14.

50   The champions would have . . . if they could have.: Haney, *Gamecock Encore*, p. 14.

51   "We weren't going to forget . . . weren't blocking very well,": Josh Kendall, "The Closer," *The State*, Sept. 11, 2011, p. 59, http://nl.newsbank.com/nl-search/we/Archives?p_action=doc&p_docid=139B274876A040.

51   It doesn't take a rocket . . . No. 21 for them.: Tim Tucker, "Freshman Marcus Lattimore Leads South Carolina Past Georgia," *ajc.com*, Sept. 11, 2010, http://www.ajc.com/sports/uga/freshman-marcus-lattimore-leads-611560.html.

52   "to have a quality at-bat . . . if you're not on base.": Neil White, "What a Blast," *The State*, June 13, 2010, http://www.thestate.com/2010/06/13/1330405/usc-coastal-game-2-updates.html.

52   He was thinking home . . . "If you see one, crush it.": White, "What a Blast."

52   "one of the better jogs . . . I touched all the bases.": White, "What a Blast."

52   We thought we had the game won. To lose it [that way] was devastating.: White, "What a Blast."

53   "No team ever won a . . . lose a title in week one.": Andy Staples, "No Thing of Beauty," *SI.com*, Aug. 31, 2012, http://sportsillustrated.cnn.com/2012/writers/andy_staples/08/31.

53   "I'll be back in there,": Staples, "No Thing of Beauty."

53   "It wasn't too pretty, but we'll take the win,": "No. 9 S. Carolina Runs to 17-13 Win over Vandy," *SI.com*, Aug. 30, 2012, http://sportsillustrated.cnn.com/football/ncaa/gameflash/2012/08/30/49679/index.html.

53   As they say in golf, never cuss a par.: Staples, "No Thing of Beauty."

54   The defensive end at . . . and where to attack.: Andy Staples, "Adding Polish to the Power," *Sports Illustrated*, Aug. 17, 2012, http://sportsillustrated.cnn.com/vault/article/magazine/MAG1202763/index.htm.

54   "I was just tiptoeing out . . . what I was supposed to do,": Staples, "Adding Polish to the Power."

54   Clowney played off a . . . toward the goal line.: Staples, "Adding Polish to the Power."

54   "If you've got an exceptional . . . through the series.: Staples, "Adding Polish to the Power."

54   His "instincts and freakish physical attributes": Staples, "Adding Polish to the Power."

54   "When God made [Clowney], he made a beast.": Staples, "Adding Polish to the Power."

54   I didn't know much last season.: Staples, "Adding Polish to the Power."

55   as his team fell behind Valparaiso 3-0,: Haney, *Gamecock Glory*, p. 31.

55 Tanner turned to his top . . . due one of these years,": Haney, *Gamecock Glory,* p. 28.

55 "There are a lot of outstanding . . . . years they'd like to forget,": Haney, *Gamecock Glory,* p. 31.

55 "had already started to. . . "dramatic and prematurely negative,": Haney, *Gamecock Glory,* p. 28.

55 Against, East Carolina, Tanner . . . this bunch didn't have "it,": Haney, *Gamecock Glory,* p. 28.

55 He never had that thought again.: Haney, *Gamecock Glory,* p. 31.

55 This could be a challenging year. It happens. It happens.: Haney, *Gamecock Glory,* p. 31.

56 The two stories recounted here were taken from an interview with Don Barton that appeared as an article titled "Don Barton's Top 10 Memories" in *The State,* Nov. 25, 2010, p. 49. It was found at http://nl.newsbank.com/nl-search/we/Archives?p_action=doc&p_docid=133B96572BE699.

56 Rex, I discovered where that phantom tackler came from.: "Don Barton's Top 10 Memories."

57 For the USC-Clemson . . . sports information department.: Willie T. Smith, "Raised in an Orange-Tinted Family," *The State,* Nov. 26, 2010, p. 24, http://nl.newsbank.com/nl-search/we/Archives?p_action=doc&p_docid=133BE78968E0727.

57 Allison saw the game as . . . as a preferred walk-on.: Smith, "Raised in an Orange-Tinted Family."

57 "I have to turn around," . . . the fans around her.: Smith, "Raised in an Orange-Tinted Family."

57 I have the rest of my . . . and support Spencer.: Smith, "Raised in an Orange-Tinted Family."

58 He instituted his own training . . . delivered the good news.: John Whittle, "Thomas Granted Sixth Year," *The Big Spur,* Feb. 2011, http://southcarolina.247sports.com/Article/Thomas-granted-sixth-year-14059.

58 "He sort of personifies what we're all about.": Neil White, "Brady Thomas: The Added Value," *2011 College World Series: Back-to-Back Champions* (Columbia: The State Media Co., 2011), p. 47.

58 I worked hard not to . . . less TD Ameritrade Park.: Haney, *Gamecock Encore,* p. 8.

59 It takes a total team effort to get in this position,": Neil White, "History-Making."

59 The five players noted as stars were designated as heroes in the 2010 world series by Neil White in "5 USC Heroes in the College World Series," *The State,* July 1, 2010, http://www.thestate.com/2010/07/01/1359092/five-usc-heroes-in-thecollege.html. The information and the direct quotes, except those noted otherwise, are taken from this article.

59 As a team, we're just as proud as we can ever be.: White, "History-Making."

60 when he spoke to his . . . pretty much the same,": Spurrier Steady in His Approach," *The State,* Nov. 12, 2010, p. 21, http://nl.newsbank. com/nl-search/we/Archives?p_action=doc&p_doicid=13374C27D3DE0F.

60 the head coach admonished . . . biggest in Gamecock history.: "Spurrier Steady in His Approach."

60 The next [game] is always . . . you have some control over.: "Spurrier Steady in His Approach."

61 "That's going to live . . . after touching home plate.: Haney, *Gamecock Encore,* p. 33.

61 his "comical-yet-not-funny" . . . had simply overslept.: Haney, *Gamecock Encore,* p. 33.

61 Head coach Ray Tanner put . . . a late defensive replacement: Haney, *Gamecock Encore,* p. 34.

61 sliding headfirst across first base: Haney, *Gamecock Encore,* p. 34.

61 I felt awful. My last game against Clemson, and I didn't even start.: Haney, *Gamecock Encore,* p. 34.

62 "the boldest possible call in such a critical time.": Haney and Williams, p. 143.

62 when the play came in, . . . guard, William "Refrigerator" Perry.: Haney and Williams, p. 143.

62 When Perry took a side, . . . opening a lane for Lewis.: Haney and Williams, p. 144.

62 "We hadn't had a sustained drive all day long,": John Boyette, "They Still Believe in the 'Magic,'" *The Augusta Chronicle*, Nov. 22, 2009, http://chronicle.augusta.com/sports/usc/2009-11-22/they-still-believe-magic.

62 We ran a trap and swung the momentum in that game.: Boyette, "They Still Believe in the 'Magic.'"

63 Prior to the game, . . . messages with Bible verses.: "Thompson Shines in Gamecocks' Win over Pirates," *scnow.com*, Sept. 9, 2012, http://www2.scnow.com/sports/pee-dee/2012//sep/08/4.

63 An excited Thompson sprinted . . . he was extremely good,": Ron Morris, "It's Official," *The State*, Sept. 9, 2012, http://www.thestate.com/2012/09/09/2433108/its-official-gamecocks-have-a.html.

63 I appreciated the 9 million Bible verses people are sending me.: Morris, "It's Official."

64 he accepted a commitment from . . . Tanner he was ready.: Neil White, "USC Has Plenty of Faith in This Christian," *The State*, Feb. 18, 2010, http:// www.thestate.com/2010/02/18/1162745/usc-has-plenty-of-faith-in-this.html.

64 ten of his family . . . get the season started.": White, "USC Has Plenty of Faith."

64 He's very mature, and he doesn't need to be mollycoddled.: White, "USC Has Plenty of Faith."

65 The celebration of the historic . . . games that clinched championships.: Ron Morris, "This Season Was the Greatest in USC History," *The State*, Jan. 3, 2012, p. 15, http://nl.newsbank.com/nl-search/we/Archives?p_action=doc&p_docid=13C0B4CE232B.

65 He gave game balls to . . . to commemorate the season.: Morris, "This Season Was the Greatest."

65 "It will have a big ol' . . . as the best team ever.": Josh Kendall, "'Best Team Ever,'" *The State*, Jan. 3, 2012, p. 15, http://nl.newsbank.com/nl-search/we/Archives?p_action=doc&p_doicid=13C0B4CE1FFE.

65 "Next year's team, they'll . . . 11 has already happened.": Kendall, "Bes t Team Ever.'"

65 We go down in history as the best team to play at Carolina.: Kendall, "'Best Team Ever.'"

66 To be a loving father, to be a loving husband and to chase after Jesus.": Crandall Sims, "Michael Roth: 'I Know Baseball Isn't Always Going to Be There,'" *ABC Columbia*, June 29, 2012, http://www.abccolumbia.com/news/local/Michael-Roth---160602955.html.

66 Roth has dreamed of . . . first threw a ball.: Darryl Slater, "USC's Roth Has Dreams," *Aiken Standard*, June 5, 2012, http://www.aikenstandard.com/story/060512-michael-roth--4047022.

66 he hasn't been regarded . . . doesn't throw particularly hard.: Slater, "USC's Roth Has Big Dreams."

66 When he was a freshman, . . . know why you're throwing.: Sims: Michael Roth."

66 he decided to return to . . . degree in international business.: Sims, "Michael Roth."

66 Roth has graduate school as a major goal.: Sims, "Michael Roth."

66 I wanna do something, . . . to "change the world.": Sims, "Michael Roth."

66 I know baseball isn't always going to be there.": Sims, "Michael Roth."

67 The players figured "they . . . couple of average games.": Haney, *Gamecock Glory*, p. 66.

67 He sent the Gamecocks out . . . like Little Leaguers,": Haney, *Gamecock Glory*, p. 67.

67 "I was about as unhappy as you could be.: Haney, *Gamecock Glory*, p. 67.

68 At that point, head coach . . . starts snapped at 28: Josh Kendall, "Off and Running," *The State*, Sept. 4, 2011, p. 53, http://nl.newsbank.com/nl-search/we/Archives?p_

GAMECOCKS

action=doc&p_docid=1398D9A5811586.

69 "Ask for more," he said. . . . to that of a manager,: Ron Morris, "The Making of a Coach," *The State*, Dec. 25, 2011, p. 21, http://nl.newsbank.com/nl-search/we/ Archives?p_action=doc&p_docid=13BDC3900.

69 Don't make excuses and don't feel sorry for yourself.: Morris, "The Making of a Coach."

70 "tentative freshman who seemed overwhelmed at times.": Neil White, "Payne Perseveres," *The State*, March 30, 2012, p. 19, http://nl.newsbank.com/nl-search/ we/Archives?p_action=doc&p_docid=13DD60BAFAB39.

70 "Absolutely not,": White, "Payne Perseveres."

70 Morales gave the youngster . . . since the tenth grade.: White, "Payne Perseveres."

71 The USC staff wasn't paying . . . drive was not one.": Haney, *Gamecock Glory*, p. 44.

71 Calvi's attitude was "show . . . which Cooper took the mound.": Haney, *Gamecock Glory*, p. 45.

71 He determined that he was done with mediocrity.: Haney, *Gamecock Glory*, p. 45.

71 So he went to work with . . . developing a cutter.: Haney, *Gamecock Glory*, p. 46.

71 He got tired of just doing OK.: Haney, *Gamecock Glory*, p. 45.

72 Rodney Paulk once said he . . . on the road for games.: Slater, Darryl, "'Life Isn't All About Football,'" *The Post and Courier*, Nov. 24, 2011, http://www.postand courier.com/article/20111124/PC20/311249921.

72 entered 2011 as an afterthought.: Josh Kendall, "Rodney Paulk: Linebacker," *Gamecocks' Greatest Season* (Columbia: The State Media Co., 2012), p. 47.

72 Rodney's a real man. . . .when you grow up.: Slater, "'Life Isn't All About Football.'"

73 "It's always been my . . . granddad played football here.": Neil White, "Following in the Family Tradition," *The State*, Aug. 18, 2011, p. 15, http://nl.newsbank.com/nl-search/we/Archives?p_action=doc&p_docid=13933EA02684A.

73 That's a cool little twist.: White, "Following in the Family Tradition."

74 "an impact player as soon as he stepped on campus.": Brittany Lane, "NFL Draft Profile: Stephon Gilmore," *Spurs Up Blog*, April 26, 2012, http://www.gamecocks online.com/blog/2012/04/nfl-profile-stephon-gilmore.html.

74 On Gilmore's left arm is a . . . with a football in his hands.": Joseph Person, "Gamecocks' Gilmore Wise Beyond His Years," *The State*, Nov. 22, 2009, http://www. thestate.com/2009/11/22/1038744/gamecocks-gilmore-wise-beyond.html.

74 "I didn't want to go . . . close to my family.": Person, "Gamecocks' Gilmore Wise."

74 I love my family. I wanted to always stay close to them.: Person, "Gamecocks' Gilmore Wise."

75 "I don't think he ever thought, 'I'm going to play,'": Josh Kendall, "Matulis Earns Another Start at Right Tackle," *The State*, Nov. 17, 2011, p. 17, http://nl.newsbank.com/nl-search/we/Archives?p_action=doc&p_doicid= 13B13FA18927C.

75 "You just can't flip . . . give Matulis another chance.: Kendall, "Matulis Earns Another Start."

75 We don't need to be . . . had around here.: Kendall, "Matulis Earns Another Start."

76 were described by one writer as "lifeless": Neil White, "USC Finds Rally Remedy," *The State*, April 14, 2012, p. 21, http://nl.newsbank.com/nl-search/we/ Archives?p_action=doc&p_docid=13E2578EFA6386.

76 "I was just trying to get on base and keep the inning going,": White, "USC Finds Rally Remedy."

76 In the seventh inning,: White, "USC Finds Rally Remedy."

76 Tanner warned little-used . . . to be ready.: White, "USC Finds Rally Remedy."

76 He's been one of the . . . dugout the entire season.: White, "USC Finds Rally Remedy."

77 Coach Chad Holbrook's list is found in Travis Haney's *Gamecock*

195

   Encore, pp. 141-42.

77   "an absolutely huge accomplishment.": Haney, *Gamecock Encore*, p. 141.

77   a win that made head coach Ray Tanner so proud he teared up: Haney, *Gamecock Encore*, p. 141.

77   "watching the best center fielder . . . tracking the last fly ball,": Haney, *Gamecock Encore*, p. 142.

78   Two seasons in Washington . . . he preferred the college game.: Rich Kaipust, "South Carolina's Spurrier Defies Age, Critics," *Omaha World-Herald*, Dec. 19, 2011, http://www.omaha.com/article/2011219/BIGRED/72199880.

78   "Some of my buddies . . . arrived in Columbia in 1999.: Kaipust, "South Carolina's Spurrier."

78   "If you go to a big . . . else already has done.: Kaipust, "South Carolina's Spurrier."

78   "We're not quite there yet,": Kaipust, "South Carolina's Spurrier."

78   The possibilities here are just endless.: Kaipust, "South Carolina's Spurrier."

79   the Gamecocks flew home . . . here was just phenomenal." Joseph Person, "Gamecock Love-In," *National Champions* (Columbia: The State Media Co., 2010), p. 72.

79   Fans eager to show their . . . the 2-1 clincher against UCLA.: "Over 13,000 Fans Celebrate CWS Title," *ESPN*, July 1, 2010, http://sports.espn.go.com/ncaa/news/story?id=5344787.

79   entered the arena to the . . . for a victory lap.: Person, "Gamecock Love-In," p. 72.

79   "It's wild in here," . . . "It's really amazing.": "Over 13,000 Fans Celebrate CWS Title."

79   Other Gamecock coaches were . . . add Tanner to the club.: Person, "Gamecock Love-In," pp. 72-73.

79   "I'm going to say it . . . "the dream of dreams.": Person, "Gamecock Love-In," p. 73.

79   It was like suddenly . . . sins are forgiven.: Person, "Gamecock Love-In," p. 73.

80   "its stingiest performance in 35 years.": Andrew Shain, "Kentucky Goes Nowhere Fast," *The State*, Oct. 9, 2011, p. 62, http://nl.newsbank.com/nl-search/we/Archives?p_action=doc&p_docid=13A4571542CF64.

80   Ugly is how you describe it. It was ugly, especially offensively.: Chris Dearing, "Wildcats Have No Answers Against USC," *The State*, Oct. 9, 2011, p. 64, http://nl.newsbank.com/nl-search/we/Archives?p_action=doc&p_docid=13A457154604D5.

81   The most common story for the . . . get rid of the Curse forever.": Roy Welsh, "'Chicken Curse' Continues to Plague Gamecocks," Jan. 27, 2006, http://bradygriffin.wordpress.com/2009/09/14/the-chicken-curse.

81   It forever "changed the image . . . the attitude of its fans.": Darryl Slater, "South Carolina's Three-Year Run of Baseball Success Forever Changed Gamecocks' Image," *The Post and Courier*, July 31, 2012, http://www.postandcourier.com/article/20120731/PC20/120739867/1037.

81   Well, that curse is gone.: Slater, "South Carolina's Three-Year Run of Baseball Success."

82   In the fall of 2008 in . . . for the rest of his life,: Haney, *Gamecock Glory*, p. 55.

82   in the fall of 2009, Holbrook . . . to avoid chasing them.: Haney, *Gamecock Glory*, p. 56.

82   But the juniors and seniors . . . adapt his hitting style.: Haney, *Gamecock Glory*, p. 57.

82   I pick up stuff real quick.: Haney, *Gamecock Glory*, p. 57.

83   living with his mom through . . . the street, point-blank period,": Joseph Person, "Devotion of Watkins, Berry Goes Beyond Blood," *The State*, Oct. 29, 2009, http://www.thestate.com/2009/10/29/1003939/devotion-of-watkins-berry.html.

83   "I was a real bad . . . basically got me straight,": Person, "Devotion of Watkins, Berry."

83   "I don't like those guys right, now,": Person, "Devotion of Watkins, Berry."

83   He always had my back, . . . as friends and brothers.: Person, "Devotion of Watkins, Berry."

84   The Gamecocks needed only eighteen minutes: Neil White, "Gamecocks Write Two

Wild Endings," *The State*, April 28, 2012, p. 19, http://nl.newsbank.com/nl-search/we/Archives?p_action=doc&p_docid=13E6F4ECC72AE2.

84 "We get one hit . . . It's just crazy.": White, "Gamecocks Write Two Wild Endings."

84 On the way to the . . . especially on one day.": White, "Gamecocks Write Two Wild Endings."

85 as he grew to be 6-1 . . . when she took gymnastics.: Darryl Slater, "Coach's Advice Helped South Carolina Defensive End Melvin Ingram," *The Post and Courier*, April 26, 2012. http://www.postandcourier.com/article/20120426/PC20/120429414/1037.

85 he called Ingram into . . . student in the classroom.: Slater, "Coach's Advice Helped."

86 "might require an increase in cap size.": Eric Boynton, "USC's Merrifield Soaking Up Sights in Omaha," *GoUpstate.com*, June 27, 2010, http://www.goupstate.com/article/20100627/news/100629719.

86 Andrews "asked me after . . . victory for me this year,': Boynton, "USC's Merrifield Soaking Up Sights."

86 I'm fine now, and after . . . so it wasn't a total loss.: Boynton, "USC's Merrifield Soaking Up Sights."

87 Del Wilkes, a freshman linebacker . . . of a Heisman winner.": Andrew Shain, "Handle with Care," *The State*, Dec. 12, 2010, p. 27, http://nl.newsback.com/nl-search/we/Archives?p_action=doc&p_docid=134137008F60AD.

87 When he won it, the . . . message to young people.: Shain, "Handle with Care."

87 '"Some of the boys, . . . even as I start talking.": Shain, "Handle with Care."

87 I won the Heisman, . . . to fall through the cracks.: Shain, "Handle with Care."

88 "all the way to the finish line of the two-week marathon.": Ryan McGee, "Omaha Falls in Love with South Carolina," *ESPN The Magazine*, June 29, 2011, http://sports.espn.go/ncaa/news/story?id=6715434.

88 "The city's mysterious selection . . . "It just happens.': McGee, "Omaha Falls in Love."

88 "unabashedly cheered for the South Carolina Gamecocks.": McGee, "Omaha Falls in Love."

88 "They're just easy to pull . . . felt like a home game.": McGee, "Omaha Falls in Love."

88 They really did, didn't they?": McGee, "Omaha Falls in Love."

89 "I've never won a game . . . we won the game.": Neil White, "11 Things Heard Throughout the Season," *Gamecocks' Greatest Season* (Columbia: The State Media Co., 2011), p. 18.

89 "If you have a big . . . get this one behind us.": Josh Kendall, "Lattimore, Gamecocks Sink Midshipmen," *GoGamecocks.com*, Sept. 18, 2011, http://www.gogamecocks.com/2011/09/18/154930/ggf-usc-vs-navy.html.

89 I've lost enough three . . . Happy to get a win.: Kendall, "Lattimore, Gamecocks Sink Midshipmen."

90 As the veteran head coach . . . and pack for a week.": Ron Morris, "SEC Tournament Not High on Priority List," *The State*, May 23, 2012, p. 19, http://nl.newsbank.com/nl-search/we/Archives?p_action=doc&p_docid=13EF3389ABA065.

90 This was the same program . . . games than anybody else.: Morris, "SEC Tournament Not High on Priority List."

90 Tanner's light suitcase thus . . . about the SEC tournament.: Morris, "SEC Tournament Not High on Priority List."

90 It would be awesome to win . . . than the SEC Tournament.: Morris, "SEC Tournament Not High on Priority List."

91 Roth talked his way back . . . it was poetic justice,": "Roth, Gamecocks Shut Out Sooners," *scnow.com*, June 9, 2012, http://www2.scnow.com/sports/2012/jun/09.

91 It was classic Roth.: "Roth, Gamecocks Shut Out Sooners."

BIBLIOGRAPHY

"Baseball Champs South Carolina Defied Steep Odds." *NPR.org.* 29 June 2011. http://www.npr.org/2011/06/29/137496223.

Boyette. John. "They Still Believe in the 'Magic.'" *The Augusta Chronicle.* 22 Nov. 2009. http://chronicle.augusta.com/sports/usc/2009-11-22/they-still-believe-magic.

Boynton, Eric. "USC's Merrifield Soaking Up Sights in Omaha." GoUpstate.com. 27 June 2010. http://www.goupstate.com/article/20100627/news/100629719.

Chatelain, Dirk. "Give Up? Boy Didn't, and His Team Hasn't." *Omaha World-Herald.* 21 June 2011. http://omaha.com/article/20110621/CWS/706219822.

Cloninger, David. "Williams Enters Hero Territory." *GamecockCentral.com.* 28 June 2011. http://southcarolinarivals.com/content.asp?CID=1235578.

Conn, Jordan. "Jeffery's Success Extra Sweet with Hometown South Carolina Team." *SI.com.* 22 July 2011. http://sportsillustrated.cnn.com/2011/writers/jordan_conn/07/22.

Connolly, Matt. "USC Defensive Lineman Ingram Says 'I Try to Do It All.'" *Go Upstate.com.* 10 Sept. 2011. http://www.goupstate.com/article/20110910/ARTICLES/110919986.

"David Roth, Father of South Carolina Pitcher Michael Roth, Quits Job to See Son Pitch." *HuffPost Sports.* 20 June 2011. http://www.huffingtonpost.com/201/06/21/david-roth-quits.

Dearing, Chris. "Belcher Starts Anew." *The State.* 11 April 2012. 17. http://l.newsbank.com/nl-search/we/Archives?p_action=doc*p_docid=13D15A0CDBDA.

———. "Wildcats Have No Answers Against USC." *The State.* 9 Oct. 2011. 64. http://nl.newsbank.com/nl-search/we/Archives?p_action=doc&p_docid=13A457154604D5.

"Don Barton's Top 10 Memories." *The State.* 25 Nov. 2010. 49. http://nl.newsbank.com/nl-search/we/Archives?p_action=doc&p_docid=133B965721BE699.

"Facilities: Carolina Stadium." *South Carolina Gamecocks.* http://www.gamecocksonline.com/facilities/carolina-stadium.html.

"GamecockCentral Says Jake Williams Won't Be on USC Baseball Team." *TheTandD.com.* 16 Feb. 2012. http://thetandd.com/sports/gamecockcentral-says.

"Gamecocks Headed Back to Title Series." *scnow.com.* 23 June 2012. http://www2.scnow.com/sports/2012/jun/5/gamecocks-headed-back-title-series-ar-4024696.

Haney, Travis. "Bayler Teal Was South Carolina's Talisman." *The New York Times.* 11 June 2011. http://www.nytimes.com/2011/06/12/sports/bayler-teal-was-south-carolinas-talisman.html.

———. *Gamecock Encore: The 2011 University of South Carolina Baseball Team's Run to Back-to-Back NCAA Championships.* Charleston: The History Press, 2012.

———. *Gamecock Glory: The University of South Carolina Baseball Team's Journey to the 2010 NCAA Championship.* Charleston: The History Press, 2011.

Haney, Travis and Larry Williams. *Classic Clashes of the Carolina-Clemson Football Rivalry: A State of Disunion.* Charleston: The History Press, 2011.

Juback, Bob. "Former Gamecock Remembers 'The Catch.'" *scnow.com.* 8 Sept. 2011. http://www2.scnow.com/sports/2011/sep/08/former-gamecock-remembers-catch-ar-2379353.

Kaipust, Rich. "South Carolina's Spurrier Defies Age, Critics." *Omaha World-Herald.* 19 Dec. 2011. http://www.omaham.com/article/2011219/BIGRED/712199880.

Kendall, Josh. "A Little Bit Rocky." *The State*. 20 Nov. 2010. 57. http://nl.newsbank.com/
    nl-search/we/Archives?p_action=doc&p_docid=1339EEC933DB92.

---. "A Man of Action." *The State*. 1 Sept.2011. 21. http://nl.newsbank.com/nl-search/
    we/Archives?p_action=doc&p_docid=1397DCD384AA.

---. "'Best Team Ever.'" *The State*. 3 Jan. 2012. 15. http://nl.newsbank.com/nl-search/
    we/Archives?p_action=doc&p_docid=13C0B4CE1FFE.

---. "Defense Dominates." *The State*. 25 Sept. 2011. 59. http://nl.newsbank.com/nl-
    search/we/Archives?p_action=doc&p_docid=139FBEE0DD4B.

---. "Finally, History." *The State*. 14 Nov. 2010. 75. http://nl.newsbank.com/nl-search/
    we/Archives?p_action=doc&p_docid=1337F533629CA05.

---. "Lattimore, Gamecocks Sink Midshipmen." *GoGamecocks.com*. 18 Sept. 2011. http:
    //www.gogamecocks.com/2011/09/18/154930/ggf-usc-vs-navy-html.

---. "Matulis Earns Another Start at Right Tackle." *The State*. 17 Nov. 2011. 17. http:
    //nl.newsbank.com/nl-search/we/Archives?p_action=doc&p_docid=
    13B13FA18927C.

---. "Military Stay Suits Quarles." *The State*. 1 Nov. 2011. 13. http://nl.newsbank.com/
    nl-search/we/Archives?p_action=doc&p_docid=13ABF40991ED.

---. "Off and Running." *The State*. 4 Sept. 2011. 53. http://nl.newsbank.com/nl-search/
    we/Archives?p_action=doc&p_docid=1398D9A5811586.

---. "Rodney Paulk: Linebacker." *Gamecocks' Greatest Season*. Columbia: The State
    Media Co. 47.

---. "Tackling a Tough Task." *The State*. 14 Sept. 2010. 15. http://nl.newsbank.com/nl-
    search/we/Archives?p_action=doc&p_docid=1323DB285EC56.

---. "Taylor Gladly Drops Back." *The State*. 28 Dec. 2010. 13. http://nl.newsbank.com/
    nl-search/we/Archives?p_action=doc&p_docid=1346794BB28D8B.

---. "The Closer." *The State*. 11 Sept. 2011. 59. http://nl.newsbank.com/nl-search/we/
    Archives?p_action=doc&p_docid=139B274876A040.

---. "The Long and Winding Road." *The State*. 30 Oct. 2010. 47. http://nl.newsbank.
    com/nl-search/we/Archives?p_action=doc&p_docid=13330517EB099F.

---. "Ward Takes Charge." *The State*. 28 Dec. 2011. 19. http://nl.newsbank.com/nl-
    search/we/Archives?p_action=doc&p_docid=13BEC29F901901.

---. "Wild Week for Shaw's Family." *The State*. 5 Sept. 2010. 21. http://nl.newsbank.
    com/nl-search/we/Archives?p_action=doc&p_doicid=1320DE168E41A.

Kratch, James. "Marty Markett Put on Scholarship." *The Daily Gamecock*. 21 Aug. 2011.
    http://www.dailygamecock.com/sports/item/1728.

Lane, Brittany. "NFL Draft Profile: Stephon Gilmore." *Spurs Up Blog*. 26 April 2012.
    http://www.gamecocksonline.com/blog/2012/04/nfl-profile-stephon-gilmore.
    html.

Langford, Richard. "Despite Injury Christian Walker Helps Lead South Carolina
    Baseball." *BleacherReport.com*. 3 June 2011. http://bleacherreport.com/
    articles/722716-college-baseball-world-series.

---. "South Carolina Baseball's Christian Walker Is Dealing with Increasing Pain
    in Wrist." *BleacherReport.com*. 3 June 2011. http://bleacherreport.com/
    articles/722716-college-baseball-world-series.

MacArthur, John. *Twelve Ordinary Men*. Nashville: W Publishing Group, 2002.

McGee, Ryan. "Omaha Falls in Love with South Carolina." *ESPN The Magazine*. 29
    June 2011. http://sports.espn.go.com/ncaa/news/story?id=6715434.

McNeal, Stan. "Cardinals Manager Mike Matheny Doesn't Want
    Anyone's Pity." *Sporting News*. 15 June 2012. http://aol.sporting

news.com/mlb/story/2012-06-15.

Morris, Ron. "A Story Lost in History." *The State*. 5 Sept. 2010. 21. http://nl.newsbank.
    com/nl-search/we/Archives?p_action=doc&p_docid=1320DE1680E962.

---. "Against All Odds, Gamecocks Find a Way to Win." *The State*. 16 Oct. 2011. 63.
    http://nl.newsbank.com/nl-search/we/Archives?p_action=doc&p_docid=
    13A6A907D783D.

---. "Curse Killers." *The State*. 20 Nov. 2010. 48. http://nl.newsbank.com/nl-search/we/
    Archives?p_action=doc&p_docid=1339EEC921120C.

---. "It's Official: Gamecocks Have a Backup QB." *The State*. 9 Sept. 2012. http://www.
    thestate.com/2012/09/09/2433108/its-official-gamecocks-have-a.html.

---. "SEC Tournament Not High on Priority List." *The State*. 23 May 2012. 19. http://
    www.nl.newsbank.com/nl-search/we/Archives?p_action=doc&p_docid=
    13EF3389ABA065.

---. "Something to Celebrate." *The State*. 15 Nov. 2010. 15. http://nl.newsbank.com/nl-
    search/we/Archives?p_action=doc&p_docid=133847CD1F6C11.

---. "Success Arrives Once Nerves Settle." *The State*. 18 Feb. 2012. 23. http://nl.news
    bank.com/nl-search/we/Archives?p_action=doc&p_docid=13CFDE241C42D9.

---. "The Making of a Coach." *The State*. 25 Dec. 201. 21. http://nl.newsbank.com/nl-
    search/we/Archives?p_action=doc&p_docid=13BDC3900.

---. "This Season Was the Greatest in USC History." *The State*. 3 Jan. 2012. 15. http:
    //nl.newsbank.com/nl-search/we/Archives?p_action=doc&p_docid=
    13C0B4CE232B.

"No. 9 S. Carolina Runs to 17-13 Win over Vandy." *SI.com*. 30 Aug. 2012. http://sports
    illustrated.cnn.com/football/ncaa/gameflash/2012/08/30/49679/index.html.

"Over 13,000 Fans Celebrate CWS Title." *ESPN*. 1 July 2010. http://sports.espn.go.com/
    ncaa/news/story?id=5344787.

Person, Joseph. "Devotion of Watkins, Berry Goes Beyond Blood." *The State*. 29 Oct.
    2009. http://www.thestate.com/2009/10/29/1003939/devotion-of-watkins-berry-
    goes.html.

---. "Gamecock Love-In: National Champs Come Home." *National Champions*.
    Columbia: The State Media Co., 2010. 72-73.

---. "Gamecocks' Gilmore Wise Beyond His Years." *The State*. 22 Nov. 2009. http://
    www.thestate.com/2009/11/22/1038744/gamecocks-gilmore-wise-beyond.html.

Roberts, Alex. "South Carolina Gamecock Marty Markett: From Walk-on to the
    NFL." *Bleacher Report*. 30 April 2012. http://bleacherreport.com/articles/
    1166532.

"Roth, Gamecocks Shut Out Sooners in First Game of Super Regional." *scnow.com*.
    9 June 2012. http://www2.scnow.com/sports/2012/jun/09.

Senkiw, Brad. "Roth's Dad Quits Job to See Son Pitch in Omaha." *Anderson Indepen-
    dent Mail*. 21 June 2011. http://www.independentmail.com/news/2011/jun/21.

Shain, Andrew. "Handle with Care." *The State*. 12 Dec. 2010. 27. http://nl.newsback.
    com/nl-search/we/Archives?p_action=doc&p_doicid=134137008F60AD.

---. "Kentucky Goes Nowhere Fast." *The State*. 9 Oct. 2011. 62. http://nl.newsbank.com
    /nl-search/we/Archives?p_action=doc&p_docid=13A4571542CF64.

---. "Spreading Blessings." *The State*. 24 Dec. 2010. 19. http://nl.newsback.com/nl-
    search/we/Archives?p_action=doc&p_doicid=1452603A115AE.

Sims, Crandall. "Michael Roth: 'I Know Baseball Isn't Always Going to Be There.'"
    ABC Columbia. 29 June 2012. http://www.abccolumbia.com/local/Michael-
    Roth---160602955.html.

Slater, Darryl. "Coach's Advice Helped South Carolina Defensive End Melvin Ingram Become a First-Round NFL Draft Pick." *The Post and Courier.* 26 April 2012. http://www.postandcourier.com/article/20120426PC20/120429414/1037.

---. "'Life Isn't All About Football'; USC's Paulk Stays Focused." *The Post and Courier.* 24 Nov. 2011. http://www.postandcourier.com/article/20111124/PC20/11249921.

---. "South Carolina Punter Tyler Hull Already Making Impact." *The Post and Courier.* 15 Aug. 2012. http://www.postandcourier.com/apps.pbcs.dll/article.

---. "South Carolina's Three-Year Run of Baseball Success Forever Changed Gamecocks' Image." *The Post and Courier.* 31 July 2012. http://www.postandcourier.com/article/200731/PC20/120739867/1037.

---. "USC's Roth Has Big Dreams On, Off Baseball Field." *Aiken Standard.* 5 June 2012. http://www.aikenstandard.com/story/060512-michael-roth--4047022.

Smith, Willie T. "Raised in an Orange-Tinted Family." *The State.* 26 Nov. 2010. 24. http://nl.newsbank.com/nl-search/we/Archives?p_action=doc&p_docid=133BE78968E0727.

"Spurrier Steady in His Approach." *The State.* 12 Nov. 2010. 21. http://nl.newsbank.com/nl-search/we/Archives?p_action=doc&p_docid=13374C27D3DE0F.

Staples, Andy. "Adding Polish to the Power." *Sports Illustrated.* 17 Aug. 2012. http://sportsillustrated.cnn.com/vault/article/magazine/MAG1202763/index.htm.

---. "No Thing of Beauty, But Gamecocks Survive Resilient 'Dores in Opener." *SI.com.* 31 Aug. 2012. http://sportsillustrated.cnn.com/2012/writers/andy_staples/08/31.

"Thompson Shines in Gamecocks' Win over Pirates." *scnow.com.* 9 Sept. 2012. http://www2.scnow.com/sports/pee-dee/2012/sep/08/4.

Tucker, Tim. "Freshman Marcus Lattimore Leads South Carolina Past Georgia." *ajc.com.* 11 Sept. 2010. http://www.ajc.com/sports/uga/freshman-marcus-lattimore-leads-611560.html.

Velasquez, Ryan. "Wilds Thing: Brandon Wilds Helps Carry Gamecocks to Win in First Career Start." *The Daily Gamecock.* 29 Oct. 2011. http://www.dailygamecock.com/sports/item/2659-gamecocks-wilds-run-past-tennessee-14-3.

Welsh, Roy. "'Chicken Curse' Continues to Plague Gamecocks." 27 Jan. 2006. http://bradygriffin.wordpress.com/2009/09/14/the-chicken-curse.

White, Neil. "5 USC Heroes in the College World Series." *The State.* 1 July 2010. http://www.thestate.com/2010/07/01/1359092/five-usc-heroes-in-thecollege.html.

---. "11 Things Heard Throughout the Season." *Gamecocks' Greatest Season.* Columbia: The State Media Co., 2011. 18-19.

---. "Brady Thomas: The Added Value." *2011 College World Series: Back-to-Back Champions.* Columbia: The State Media Co., 2011. 47.

---. "Defense Shows Its Teeth." *The State.* 25 Sept. 2011. 60. http://nl.newsbank.com/nl-search/we/Archives?p_action=doc&p_docid=139FBEE0E281A.

---. "Enders Gains Control Behind Home Plate." *The State.* 2 March 2010. http://www.thestate.com/2010/03/02/1182040/enders-gains-control-behind-home.html.

---. "Following in the Family Tradition." *The State.* 18 Aug. 2011. 15. http://nl.newsbank.com/nl-search/we/Archives?p_action=doc&p_docid=13933EA02684A.

---. "Gamecocks Baseball Team Still Feeling the Love." *The State.* 3 Sept. 2010. 26. http://nl.newsbank.com/nl-search/we/Archives?p_action=doc&p_docid=132035109D6C1.

---. "Gamecocks Write Two Wild Endings." *The State.* 28 April 2012. 19. http://nl.newsbank.com/nl-search/we/Archives?p_action=

doc&p_docid=13E6F4ECC72AE2.

---. "History-Making: Gamecocks Win National Title." *thestate.com*. 30 June 2010. http://www.thestate.com/2010/06/30/1356445/usc-national-champions.html.

---. "National Championship Has a Nice Ring to It." *The State*. 7 Nov. 2010. 100. http://nl.newsbank.com/nl-search/we/Archives?p_action=doc&p_docid=1335A8A0E37B30.

---. "Opening Act Is Classy Move." *The State*. 10 April 2012. 11. http://nl.newsbank.com/nl-search/we/Archives?p_action=doc&p-docid=13E109503590A19.

---. "'Our Rock, the Unheralded Superstar." *National Champions*. Columbia: The State Media Co., 2010. 51.

---. "Payne Perseveres." *The State*. 30 March 2012. 19. http://nl.newsbank.com/nl-search/we/Archives?p_action=doc&p_docid=13DD60BAFAB39.

---. "Quarles Follows Father to USC." *GoGamecocks.com*. 4 Feb. 2010. http://www.thestate.com/2010/02/04/1141154/quarles-follows-father-to-usc.html.

---. "'Storybook Ending'": USC's Coach Answers Questions About the Title Run, the Team's Future." *The State*. 11 July 2010. http://www.thestate.com/2010/07/11/1372586/storybook-ending.html.

---. "Sweet Sound of Success." *The State*. 26 Sept. 2010. 21. http://nl.newsbank.com/nl-search/we/Archives?p_action=doc&p_docid=1327CEA5BA4D.

---. "USC Finds Rally Remedy." *The State*. 14 April 2012. 21. http://nl.newsbank.com/nl-search/Archives?p_action=doc&p_docid=13E2578EFA6386.

---. "USC Has Plenty of Faith in This Christian." *The State*. 18 Feb. 2010. http://www.thestate.com/2010/02/18/1162745/usc-has-plenty-of-faith-in-this.html.

---. "Ward Rewards Faith Spurrier Put in Him." *The State*. 3 Jan. 2012. 16. http://nl.newsbank.com/nl-search/we/Archives?p_action=doc&p_docid=13C0B4CE2F78E.

---. "What a Blast: Walker's Homer Sends USC to College World Series." *The State*. 13 June 2010. http://www.thestate.com/2010/06/13/1330405/usc-coastal-game-2-updates.html.

Whittle, John. "Thomas Granted Sixth Year." *The Big Spur*. Feb. 2011. http://southcarolina.247sports.com/Article/Thomas-granted-sixth-year-14059.

GAMECOCKS

INDEX
(LAST NAME, DEVOTION DAY NUMBER)

203